Trail of
Blood

A Canadian
Murder Odyssey

Trail of
Blood

A Canadian
Murder Odyssey

Frank Jones

McGraw-Hill Ryerson Limited

Toronto   Montreal   New York   St. Louis   San Francisco
Auckland   Bogotá   Guatemala   Hamburg
Johannesburg   Lisbon   London   Madrid   Mexico
New Delhi   Panama
Paris   San Juan   Sào Paulo   Singapore   Sydney   Tokyo

TRAIL OF BLOOD

ISBN 0-07-548414-5

1 2 3 4 5 6 7 8 9 0 D 0 9 8 7 6 5 4 3 2 1

Printed and bound in Canada

Care has been taken to trace ownership of copyright material contained
in this text. The publishers will gladly take any information that will
enable them to rectify any reference or credit in subsequent editions.

Canadian Cataloguing in Publication Data

Jones, Frank, date–
    Trail of blood

ISBN 0-07-548414-5

1. Murder—Canada—Case studies.   I. Title.

HV6535.C3J66   364.1'523'0971   C81-094834-6

Contents

Prologue	vii
She Wore a Shroud	1
The Mayor They Charged with Murder	14
The Body in the River	25
The Case of the Missing Baby	36
Good-bye, Olive Swimm, and Sleep	48
Albert Guay: The Great Pretender	59
Shootout at Megantic	69
The Judge Who was Tried for Murder	80
Who Poisoned Percy Bell?	90
A Marriage of Inconvenience	98
How Anti-Semitism Saved a Toronto Killer	110
What the Children Saw	121
The Sifton Murder	134
A Strangler So Gentle	148
The Hot Stove Murder	160
Martha McCullough: Murdered in the Name of God	173
Toot, Toot, Tootsie! Goo' Bye	184
The Professor Panicked	195
Who Shot the Scottish Nightingale?	207
The Nightmare of Paul Stromkins	219

To Ayesha

Prologue

On New Year's Day 1981, I set out on a journey across Canada to gather and record information about significant murder cases. I began on Signal Hill, overlooking the Atlantic Ocean where Catherine Snow had watched the approach of spring from her cell window in 1834 knowing that soon she would be parted from her newborn baby to follow her lover, Tobias Mandeville, to the gallows.

My journey ended some two months and 18,000 kilometres later on Beacon Hill where crocuses bloomed high above the Pacific Ocean. It was here that a fisherman, Paul Stromkins, had witnessed a brutal, haunting murder at sea.

I learned along the way that murder goes beyond the act of brutal and calculating violence recorded by police statistics; frequently, a killing is the final desperate response to oppressive social conditions, and in that terrible moment when the knife is raised, the gun pointed, we see a whole society revealed. Or murder may be the final eccentricity of larger-than-life characters who later take their places in the folk songs and folklore of our country. Like it or not, murder reveals something of our national psyche.

Acts of murder are such deeply felt and dramatic occurrences in the lives of individuals and communities that they are never forgotten. Intense and cinematic, they linger in memory like black and white images of some more primitive past. When a life is taken it is as though the action is frozen: every motive, emotion and scrap of conversation is recorded, and lives that otherwise would have been passed in obscurity are, through their connection with an act of violence, illuminated for posterity.

It's not simply morbidness that gives murder its fascination: we are lured to the story for what it tells us about the human heart and about the lives of individuals. I found in my travels a richness of characters. Even though the stories are written and now behind me, I cannot erase from my mind the story of May Bannister and the cruelty of her crime, the religious fanaticism of the McCulloughs as they took the life of their child, the mute anguish of the Kendall children who could never tell anyone what had happened to their mother . . . and so much more.

I read trial transcripts, newspaper accounts, local histories, and wherever possible visited the murder scenes and talked to anyone having a connection with the crimes. I was overwhelmed by the assistance I received from many policemen, both active and retired, from those who participated to a greater or lesser degree in the dramas and from historians, folklorists, archivists, librarians and journalists.

I would like to extend my thanks to just a few of the many who were outstanding in their helpfulness: Paul O'Neill in St. John's, Newfoundland; Ian MacNeil and John Campbell in Sydney, Nova Scotia; Allan Rankin and Larry LeClair in Charlottetown, Prince Edward Island; J. Edward "Ned" Beliveau in Shediak, New Brunswick; Ken MacLaughlen and Marion Lindsay in Woodstock, New Brunswick; Robert McKenzie in Quebec City; Roger

Lemelin in Montreal; Winnifred Inderwick in Perth, Ontario; Noel Moore, Superintendent Geoff Cooper, Commissioner Harold Graham, Gwyn "Jocko" Thomas, Sergeant Ernest Pollock, Linden MacIntyre, Steve Speisman and the Honourable J.C. McRuer in Toronto; Staff Sergeant George Paterson in Guelph, Ontario; Inspector Donald Andrews and Orlo Miller in London, Ontario; Eric Wells and George Blow in Winnipeg, Manitoba; Peter Darke and Bruce Peacock in Regina, Saskatchewan; David J. Carter in Calgary, Alberta; Shirley Kolanchey in Edmonton, Alberta; Cecil "Nobby" Clark in Victoria, British Columbia.

I am especially grateful to my editors at the *Toronto Star* for financing what must have seemed a somewhat bizarre enterprise and, in particular, John Miller and Geoff Chapman, editors of the *Sunday Star*.

Frank Jones
Toronto, April 1981

She Wore a Shroud

I stood on the shore of Conception Bay, on the rock where the murder took place, and in the cry of a gull I heard again Catherine Snow's last cry as she looked in the mirror and saw herself dressed in a shroud. The waves below gurgled, the pebbles rattled, and my eyes swung up to Spectacle Hill where the two decaying corpses, one her lover, had hung in their chains.

Some think Newfoundland a bleak place. But Conception Bay, west of St. John's, in the early part of the last century offered as lively a scene of human activity as could be found in the British Empire. In little towns with names like Blow Me Down and Bareneed clinging to the sides of eccentric hills like limpets to the back of a sea serpent, thousands of people arriving from the United Kingdom and Ireland entered a life of ceaseless challenge, harvesting the richest fishery in the world. On seas bristling with small boats, they courted the comely cod, caught 'em, split 'em, salted 'em, dried 'em in the sun, barreled 'em up and shipped 'em off to feed the world.

It was in such a landscape that there occurred 150

years ago a murder as Gothic as anything the Brontës could have imagined and yet completely modern in its central theme: the love of a young man and an older woman. The victim's name was John Snow, and his death leaves us with an interesting conundrum: was Catherine, Snow's wife, hanged for murder—or for adultery?

Certainly Catherine's actions following the murder of her husband on the fishing stage near their home on August 31, 1833, were suspicious, but even Chief Justice Henry Bolton, a harsh, side-whiskered conservative known as "the hanging judge," said there was nothing in the evidence to implicate her in the act of murder. Was the verdict of the all-male jury, then, an expression of their censure for Catherine's undignified affair with a man almost half her age?

Today we would call it a fashionable dalliance; but in the context of the times their affair offended decency and propriety. Catherine, fortyish and plain, was a matron with seven children and a house to keep for her modestly well-off husband John, a planter (or landowner) at Salmon Cove near Port de Grave. Tobias Mandeville, aged twenty-three, was a handsome, muscular master cooper who came to ply his barrel-making craft for Messrs. Martin and Jacob, merchants at nearby Bareneed. The year was 1832.

It was not long before the engaging Mandeville was asked by John Snow to come over every Saturday night for supper and to do the account books. Soon Catherine found herself looking forward to these Saturday night visits when, looking up from her sewing, she could surreptitiously admire Tobias Mandeville's strong shoulders and curly head bent over the account books.

On October 8 that year, a sunny, early fall day with the air pungent and wine-sharp, Catherine, her husband away fishing, had to walk over the hills to Harbour Grace on some errands. Tobias offered to go with her.

"Wait! Wait for me," she gasped, as he strode up the hill ahead of her. "I'm not a girl, you know, Toby. I can't run the way I used to."

He turned with a smile. "Oh, to me you are a girl all right. And you will always be."

She blushed. "Well, dear soul, when I am with you, I feel I am young again. It's as if the rest of it, the house, the children, are not there any more. Bless me, what am I saying," she said, laughing.

"Catherine," he said, his strong arm around her waist as they walked, "I only wish that I had been the first to love you." When they stopped again to catch their breath, he pulled her to him, and when he kissed her she kissed him back. And when they tumbled into the bracken, the sharp smell of the growth enveloping them, she held him to her tight.

There was no remorse. While later in the cold and disapproving language of the courtroom their act would be called "a criminal connexion," for Tobias and Catherine it was an experience that drove them to seek each other at every opportunity during the next two years.

With maids around the house and children forever underfoot, they were hard put to be alone. But there were some occasions when John Snow was away fishing that they met in the woods, separation making their kisses and the eager joining of their bodies all the more urgent and fulfilling.

"Now why would you be wasting your time with a woman of my age with so many girls to choose from?" she would taunt.

"Love of my heart, there's no one holds a candle to you," he'd say. "You're all I want in this life and the next."

"Ah, Tobias, what future is there in it for us? For I am tied and that's for sure."

"Tied you are, but if John were not here I would marry you in a flash, I would too."

Although John Snow showed no sign of knowing of the relationship, and continued to invite Tobias to his home to do the books, relations between John and Catherine deteriorated, and by the summer of 1833 they verged on violence.

"I'll have your skull broken for that," she shouted at him one day in the bedroom of their two-storey home, a home grand enough to have a separate servants' stairway.

"Will you, now?" he snarled, ripping the bonnet from her head.

Catherine was to claim later that she went in fear of John's violent temper. But on August 31, a Saturday that started out squally and cool, we find Catherine and John on passable terms. And later in the day, when the sky clears and the sea moderates, Catherine offers to help her husband take a boatload of dried cod to the Martin and Jacob warehouse a kilometre away at Bareneed. Catherine's motive was to steal a few moments with her beloved in Bareneed and, as the jury would be told, it was during those few moments that the murder plot was set in place.

The day had become beautiful, the temperature 15°C— balmy by Newfoundland standards—and, as the Snows sailed home, a red sun was setting over the humpback hills and rocky coves of Conception Bay. It was to be the last sunset John Snow would see.

Later, Snow returned to Bareneed alone in his boat to pick up Mandeville for the customary Saturday evening supper. After arriving back at Salmon Cove, and while Snow tied up the boat, Mandeville nimbly ran up the ladder leading to the fishing stage—a platform on stilts perched high on the rock out of reach of the pounding waves. Waiting to meet him in the shadows stood Arthur Spring, a twenty-eight-year-old Irish servant of the Snows, nervously grasping his master's loaded gun. In the next few moments the two men were close to panic as they waited for Snow to climb the ladder, knowing what they must do.

They heard Snow's boots on the rungs, the heavy breathing as the burly planter heaved himself up, saw his head appearing over the edge of the stage. Unsuspecting, Snow hauled himself onto the stage, took a few steps forward, then gaped as a man came out of the shadows pointing a gun at his chest. The barrel blazed in the darkness and Snow fell dead without a groan.

Weak and shaking, Spring grasped Mandeville's hand. "Isn't that well done!" he said. Hastily they tied a rope under Snow's arms and lowered him over the edge of the stage until they heard the weight splash dully in the water. They ran down the ladder, jumped into the boat and rowed out into the harbour, towing the half-submerged corpse behind them.

"This'll do," came one voice in the darkness. They hauled the body to the side of the boat, attached an iron grapnel and dropped it gently over the side. The water swirled and bubbled, and the body sank out of sight. "They'll never find him. He's forty fathoms down," whispered the other.

At the Snow house that night, life had been reassuringly normal. After the master left to get Mandeville, the maid, Kit White, had supper with the five Snow children then living at home.

"Why don't you go over to William Hele's wake? You could take Bridget and Eliza [the two oldest daughters, sixteen and seventeen]," Catherine suggested to Kit. Mary Connolly, another servant girl, might go too, she said.

"I don't know, mistress, my foot hurts me so," said Kit, making a pained face.

"Well, here, take one of my shoes. It will not pinch so," said Catherine, slipping off one of her own shoes and giving it to Kit.

Mary said she had already been to the wake at nearby Cupids the two previous nights, but at Catherine's urging the four girls finally left. Later Mandeville and Snow, after having supper, joined the girls at the wake, bringing them home at about 3:00 A.M. Kit was surprised to find no light in the house and the fire gone out. Two of the younger children were in bed, but no one else was at home. She sent Bridget to the nearby house of John Snow's brother, Edward, to get tinder to light the fire, while Mandeville and Spring returned to the wake.

The next morning, Catherine, who had spent the night with Ruth Snow, her sister-in-law (Edward being away in the Labrador fishery), came bustling home and seemed surprised that her husband was not there. He'd been in a terrible mood the night before, she said, and she'd taken the smallest child with her over to Ruth's in fear. The last she'd heard of her husband, he'd been chasing some pigs from their door just as she went into Ruth's house.

With Mandeville, Spring, her daughters and the neighbours, she began searching for John Snow. It wasn't long before they noticed his boat loose and bumping gently against the rocks in the harbour. And cod stacked on a flake had been strewn about, as though by vandals or thieves. It was suspected that Snow had either been killed by strangers or had committed suicide.

But his old friend, the Bareneed merchant John Jacob, was not satisfied with these explanations, and possibly knowing something of Catherine Snow's affair with his employee, Jacob took his suspicions to Robert Pinsent, the Port de Grave magistrate. Constable John Bows was sent to the Snow home to investigate and met Mandeville coming from the parlour. "Mrs. Snow is going from one faint to another," he told the officer. "She's not well."

But going into the parlour, Bows found Catherine surprisingly composed, and not a little put out at what she called Magistrate Pinsent's "meddling." Catherine told Bows that on the night of the 31st she, Mandeville, Spring and her husband had sat down to supper, and on learning that Bridget and Eliza had gone to the wake, John Snow had flown into a rage.

"I'll take your life and theirs if they don't come back soon," she quoted him as saying. After Spring and Mandeville left for the wake, Snow was still ranting and taking up his gun, which he always kept loaded on the rack; he went outside and fired it into the air. Later he went for a walk and Catherine, fearing for her safety, took the smallest child and went to Ruth Snow's house for the night.

Looking around, Constable Bows noticed bloodstains on Snow's fishing stage—and fresh nicks in the wood where other stains could have been cut out. On part of the superstructure he found a long trickle of dried blood. But when he had the harbour dragged on that and succeeding days, there was no sign of the body. The search was abandoned when circling sharks seemed to tell their own story.

On September 5, Spring and Mandeville were arrested on suspicion of murder and locked up at Port de Grave in cells separated only by a thin wall of planks. Robert Pinsent positioned a constable beneath a desk next to the cells in an effort to overhear any conversation between Spring and Mandeville. Returning two hours later, he relieved the eavesdropper, but Spring, looking through a crack in the planks, detected the ploy.

"That man has been listening under the table," he shouted.

"What did he hear? What did he hear?" Mandeville cried, alarmed.

Shortly after, Spring indicated that he wanted to talk to Pinsent; his first words to the magistrate were, "We killed him. Mandeville, myself and Mrs. Snow." In a confession he claimed that Mandeville had put him up to the murder a month before, promising "good times afterwards" with the bad-tempered and disagreeable Snow out of the way.

"It would be better to give him a beating," Spring had said. He claimed Mandeville insisted that murdering him outright would be better still. Spring and his master had had many disagreements, and Snow was threatening to withhold a good part of his wages at the end of the season. Mandeville's offer to pay him full wages without deductions convinced Spring to join the murder plot.

Various plans were hatched, including a proposal to kill Snow with a hatchet, but their nerve failed them. Catherine too, Spring claimed, spoke to him about the need to kill her husband, and it was she who had given him the gun to go down to the fishing stage August 31 after sending her daughters and servants away to the wake.

He had waited for half an hour on the stage, becoming increasingly nervous. At length Mandeville came up the ladder, stepping aside to give Spring a clear field of fire. But Spring's hands trembled so much he could not pull the trigger. "I haven't the courage," he said.

"Then stand out of the way," snapped Mandeville, grabbing the gun and firing as Snow came toward them.

Later, Spring claimed, Mrs. Snow asked him to scatter fish around to make it appear as though a robbery had taken place.

"Lord have mercy on me," said Mandeville, turning to the wall as he heard that Spring's confession had implicated Catherine and himself.

That evening he told his former employer, John Jacob, that he wanted to make a clean breast of it, "so you won't think me the perfect monster." Since he had first lain with Catherine Snow two years ago, they had been thinking of murdering her husband, he said. Several times he had failed to carry out murder plans when his nerve failed him, and eventually he had entangled Spring in the plans.

Mandeville had made the final arrangements for the murder with Catherine August 31st, the afternoon she came over with her husband to Bareneed, he said. But on one point he was adamant: he had not fired the fatal shot. And, he told Jacob, "It was not for the sake of John Snow's money nor for any hatred or ill will against him, but wholly for the love of the woman that I took part in such a deed." Mandeville was to deny he had ever made this confession to John Jacob.

A few days later Tobias Mandeville and Arthur Spring were handcuffed and lashed in the bow of a boat to be taken to face trial in St. John's. "I declare to you," said Mandeville, his face white with fear at the start of a journey he sensed would end on the gallows, "as if I were in the presence of God . . . that I did not fire the gun, but this man [Spring] fired the gun."

Meanwhile Constable Bows, arriving at the Snow's home to arrest Catherine, found her gone. Men sent out to find her searched the home of her friend Mary Britt but failed to find Catherine, as she had been hiding beneath the bed. However, when Mary Britt heard the facts of the case from the police, she ordered Catherine out of her house and, with nowhere to turn, Mrs. Snow gave herself up.

She continued to insist to the magistrate that she had had no part in the killing. Her story was that on the evening of the murder Spring had taken the gun, as he often did to scare dogs away from the fish on the stage, and that she had later heard the gun discharge. When Mandeville and Spring came in, she asked them where the master was. Spring said he would soon be home. With the supper growing cold, she was worried.

"Cheer up your heart, there is nothing the matter," Mandeville was to have said, and the two men had soon afterwards left for the wake. Afraid to be on her own, Catherine had taken the smallest child to Ruth Snow's for the night. She discovered her husband was still missing when she returned in the morning.

The Snow murder occurred at a time when there was an eruption of violence in the normally peaceful and thriving colony. With the arrival of thousands of poor Irish immigrants who were fleeing famine, it was a time of social and political upheaval; there were no fewer than eight people charged with murder awaiting the assizes in January 1834.

The ranks of prisoners joined by Spring, Mandeville and Snow in gaol on Signal Hill ranged from a girl accused of murdering her illegitimate child to a man accused of killing a fellow who had refused his homosexual advances, and Judge Boulton, a former attorney-general of Upper Canada and much hated in Newfoundland, soon had them dancing on the gallows.

But in a century when women were to be submissive to their husbands' desires, few crimes inspired more shock than the crime charged against Catherine Snow; it struck at the foundations of nineteenth-century patriarchal society. As Judge Boulton explained to the jury, the charges against Spring and Catherine Snow were more serious than those laid against Tobias Mandeville. For a servant to kill his master, or a wife her husband, amounted to petty treason, equivalent in lesser degree to killing the king, he explained.

In a strikingly similar American case in Delaware 100 years earlier, the same principle of British law had been applied when Catherine Bevan was burned at the stake for the murder of her husband. Peter Murphy, a servant who took part in the murder, was merely hanged.

Judge Boulton had stated that there was nothing in Mandeville or Spring's testimony to implicate Catherine Snow in "so unnatural and horrible a crime," but the prosecuting attorney-general sent a shiver through the male jury when he spoke of a murder plan hatched for the exercise of "lustful gratification . . . by his own wife."

Testifying that Tobias Mandeville had told him he had had "criminal intercourse" with Catherine Snow the day after the murder, Constable Bows also reminded the jury of Catherine's infidelity. Further, Mary Connolly, one of the servants, testified that she had found Mandeville's blood-stained fustian trousers behind a trunk in Mrs. Snow's bedroom a few days after the murder. Never mind that Kit White said she might have put them there with a pile of washing, the jurymen shivered and remembered it.

Called on for his defence, Mandeville, in the words of a contemporary report, "appeared to lose sight of himself altogether and endeavoured, as much as lay in his power, to clear the character of the female prisoner from the criminality alluded to in the evidence. He said he must have said it [incriminated Catherine] when he was unconscious of what he was saying."

It took the jury half an hour to find the three prisoners guilty. It was 11:00 P.M. on Saturday. Judge Boulton was about to issue the court's verdict when a court official asked to speak. Catherine Snow, he said, claimed to be pregnant. A flurry of excitement went through the crowded courtroom. Slightly flustered, the judge appointed a jury of matrons to examine the prisoner. Then he put on his death cap and sentenced all three to death.

The matrons reported back that Catherine was indeed in an advanced stage of pregnancy, and Judge Boulton respited her to the next assizes. But early Monday morning, Mandeville and Spring, smartly turned out in blue jackets, white pants and matching gloves, "fine young men," according to one observer, stepped onto the gallows stage in front of the courthouse on Duckworth Street. "Mandeville made his exit from this world with very little suffering. . . . His miserable companion endured a strife with human nature for nearly three minutes before animal life became extinct," noted a local newspaper editor. On the judge's orders, the bodies were taken to Spectacle Hill and hanged in chains.

In the Signal Hill gaol, hard by Gibbet Hill where only a few years before sailors were hanged and gibbetted in chains high up over the harbour as a grisly example to other seamen, Catherine wilted and sickened. Lying in her cell, she could hear the winter gales sweep in from the Atlantic, buffeting the stone walls, and the dull roar of the waves on the cliffs below. A few weeks later, Catherine's time at hand, a midwife was summoned, and soon the cries of a newborn baby echoed from the prison's cold walls.

Catherine held the child, crying for the precious little time the child would be hers. With dread she saw the snow melt that spring, the short windblown turf grow green on the hill.

In July, the blueberries ripening just beyond the jail enclosure and the sun glittering on the sea, Catherine was again taken to the courthouse. If she had prayed that Judge Boulton had relented, her hopes were in vain. He again sentenced her to death.

Back in jail, she received her last visit from her children; the baby was taken from her. Only the Catholic clergy were with her now, and in that last week they were busy circulating a petition throughout St. John's for her reprieve, believing she was not guilty.

Her days were spent in prayer and attempts to resign herself to her fate.

"Ah, sir, is there no hope?" she asked one of the priests two days before she was to hang.

"No, my good ma'am. It is my duty to entreat you to lay aside such thoughts," he replied. "It is only in heaven your hopes are to rest." For two nights Catherine didn't sleep and refused to eat. On Sunday, the eve of her execution, the governor of the jail tried to tempt her to eat delicacies.

"Oh, what is nourishment to me!" she cried. "God calls upon me to suffer death. That, I cannot avoid. But, oh, let me add as much as possible to my suffering that I may try to make that death valuable."

At 3:00 A.M. she was offered Mass; at 5:00 came the ceremonial investment of the shroud. Looking in the mirror, she uttered a piercing scream; the priests were sure she had lost her reason. But as the hour approached she grew calm again. With three priests in attendance, she walked through the courtroom where that harsh sentence had twice been proclaimed and climbed up the steps onto the windowsill. The sashes had been removed, and the platform for the gallows built outside again. Perched on a steep hillside, the stone courthouse towered above the square where hundreds of people had gathered, many with picnic baskets.

A hush fell on the crowd as Catherine Snow stepped from between the drapes, calm and praying. It was over in a few moments, and the priests, believing her innocent, allowed friends to bury her the same day in the Catholic burial ground in St. John's.

"She died," wrote the *Newfoundlander* the next day, "declaring she was a wretched, sinful woman, but as innocent of any participation in the crime for which she was about to suffer as a child unborn and that she had not even the most distant presentiment at any time that her husband would have fallen under the hand of an assassin."

* * *

John Snow's fishing stage is gone, and lilac trees and a

few foundations mark where the house once stood. Descendants of John and Catherine Snow still live hereabouts, but prefer not to remember that dark chapter in the family history.

Newton Morgan, a high school teacher who grew up in Salmon Cove, remembers being taken as a child to the rock on which John Snow's fishing stage stood and having the bejesus scared out of him by older folks who showed him red stains and told him the blood of murder can never wash away. It was a place to sit and ponder that long-ago murder inspired by an out-of-season romance. Was Catherine Snow guilty of murder—or guilty of adultery?

"And the baby," said Newton. "Whatever happened to her baby? Someday I'm going to find out." But he'll get no help from people around here.

The Mayor They Charged
with Murder

Imagine, if you will, an affable Alfred Hitchcock and you will have a notion of Mayor D. Jack MacLean, for eight years chief magistrate of the Cape Breton steel town of Sydney, Nova Scotia. Portly, ruddy-faced Mayor MacLean was gregarious, kindly and widely loved, and it was a matter of pride to the congregation when the dignified MacLean took his seat as an elder in a front pew at Bethel Presbyterian Church.

Then one rainy Sunday night in December 1949, the phone jangled on reporter Ian MacNeil's desk at the *Post-Record*.

"You better get over to the mayor's place right away, boy," the police desk sergeant's voice rasped. "Something big is going on."

MacNeil, today the executive editor of the Cape Breton *Post*, ran the block and a half to the big green wooden house at the corner of Charlotte and Nepean. The street was Sunday quiet, and as he stood listening to the rain he began to wonder why he was there. Then he saw the mayor's familiar eight-year-old blue Plymouth come up the road. MacLean climbed unsteadily from the driver's seat and, without noticing MacNeil, made his way uncertainly up the steps and through the back door.

The next morning when John Campbell, today a reporter for the *Post*, arrived at his holiday job at Woolworths, the place was agog; rumours were flying fast and furious. "The first was that the mayor had been murdered," he recalled. At lunch break everyone ran down the road to the office of the *Post-Record* and crowded around the placard pinned up outside. If it was high drama they were seeking, they were not disappointed: "Mayor D. Jack MacLean Charged with Murder of Voting Registrar," the posting read.

Sydney had just come through a hard-fought municipal election campaign, and everyone knows that down east in the salty sea air of Nova Scotia elections have always been taken mighty seriously. Friendships are fractured, a few heads get broken, principles get a little bent, and when votes become the stuff of everyday commerce, well, it's *winning* that's important. But the murder of an electoral official—now that was something awful strong, even for a bare-knuckle town like Sydney. And it didn't take anyone very long to figure out that if the voting registrar, little crippled Joe MacKinnon, had been murdered, it was sure to be connected with the vote.

As elections go, it had been a real shindig. For all his affability, people were beginning to think that Jack MacLean hadn't done much for Sydney during his eight years. Municipal corruption and patronage in a city where services were poor and large parts of the city were without sewers and water supply moved the local Kinsmen's Club to put up one of its members, Vic Coffin, as a reform candidate against MacLean in the December 6 election. It wasn't long before Coffin was gaining fast on the fifty-eight-year-old mayor and McLean, determined to keep the job he had enjoyed so much, realized he needed something extra if he was to win.

Now it may have been completely accidental, but when they arrived at the polling booths hundreds of voters, most of them by remarkable coincidence Coffin supporters, found they had been left off the voters' list. Bruce MacDonald remembers he was one of those left off. He went down to City Hall, and there was a great long line of people who had been left off, people like doctors and the manager of the steel plant.

Some, on a selective basis, were reinstated on the list. Most, like MacDonald, who had intended voting for Coffin, were not. MacLean squeaked in with a majority of 131, and Coffin and his supporters hired a lawyer to have the election upset in court. It *just* so happened that the key figure, if it came to court battle, would be none other than the mayor's oldest and dearest friend, Joe MacKinnon, who he had known since 1911 and who he had installed as voting registrar at City Hall—the same Joe MacKinnon now lying in the morgue with a black eye, a fractured skull, seven fractured ribs and the diamond pattern of the mayor's car tires across his trousers.

That Sunday in December had begun normally enough for Mayor MacLean. He'd put on his black pinstripe suit and made his customary appearance for morning service at Bethel Church. Afterwards he'd had two or three drinks at home and asked his wife Edith if she'd like to go out for a drive to their summer cottage at Blackett's Lake, twelve kilometres outside Sydney, with Joe MacKinnon.

"No, Jack, I'm too busy wrapping the Christmas parcels," she said, so he drove across town to pick up Joe. In rugged Cape Breton where for generations getting work has too often depended on who you know, Jack MacLean had been the greatest piece of luck that had ever crossed the path of the little bookkeeper.

Wherever Jack's inventive mind took him—into the used car business, into the insurance business and finally into politics, MacLean was always MacKinnon's meal ticket. He'd brought Joe into City Hall, first in the tax collection branch, and then got him the job as voting registrar. He'd even given Joe a loan when one of the MacKinnon boys entered the priesthood.

That Sunday, Joe MacKinnon's wife was to remember, her husband was in low spirits. Vic Coffin believes to this day that MacKinnon, bothered by his conscience, had seen a priest and decided he couldn't lie in court about the voting scandal, however much his old buddy pressed him.

The two friends drove first to two "open houses" in Sydney—homes where a fellow could buy a drink any hour of the day or night—and at each they had two or three shots of rum. By about 4:00 P.M. MacLean put out of his mind his promise to be home for supper at 6:00 and turned the car towards the cottage at Blackett's Lake.

About 9:40 that evening a young man named Raider Ericson was out for a drive with his girlfriend when he heard a horn blowing and saw the blue Plymouth jammed against a post in the cottage laneway. Mayor MacLean, at the wheel, asked Ericson for a push. The youngster asked him to move over, hopped in, and drove the car from the post without any trouble. Ericson noticed that while the seat. It was dark and I could not see what it was." About the mayor's condition he was quite clear: "He was drunk." Ericson was quite certain of the time, for when he got back into his car the Red Skelton radio show was just ending.

A short time later, bus driver Charles Rutherford saw the mayor's blue Plymouth driving ahead of him along King's Road in Sydney. "It was weaving from one side to the other. Most of the time it was on the left side of the road, and several cars had to duck in to avoid it," he said. Rutherford had to crawl along behind the blue car at twenty-five kilometres per hour because he didn't dare overtake it. To his relief, the car turned into a laneway beside Matt MacQuarrie's hardware store.

Fifteen minutes later steelworker Edward Costey, waiting for a bus across the road from the hardware store, heard shouting from the laneway. He saw a car back up, hit an object, go forward, then back into a telegraph pole before speeding away.

As she sat by her kitchen window, Mrs. Dan MacAskill also heard the shouting and then the cry, "Oh, Jack!" and "Don't, Jack!" She turned off the light, lifted the blind and saw a white-haired man on the ground, a car running back and forth over him.

Twelve-year-old Margaret MacAskill, perhaps with keener ears than her mother, distinctly heard the prone figure shout, "Stop Jack! Stop Jack!" She said the car then ran over him a second time.

Leslie MacAskill and Jackie MacVicar took down the car licence number and phoned the police.

Constable Alex Goldie, now retired, was one of the first on the scene, and he found MacKinnon lying in the laneway in the pouring rain in a jackknife position, his crutch and hat lying nearby. "He was all broken, his ribs crushed," Goldie told me. He got down on his knees in the mud and put his ear right up to MacKinnon's mouth. "It was hard to understand him because his mouth was full of blood. He just said three words. 'If I die . . .' But he couldn't finish."

"If I die . . ." What might Joe MacKinnon have said if he'd only been able to finish that sentence! A few more words might have sent his old friend to the gallows for murder—or home with a judicial slap on the wrist. But it was not to be: half an hour later he died in hospital without another word.

Constable Goldie, realizing who owned the car, drove directly to the mayor's house, where he saw the blue car parked out back. "I felt the radiator, and it was still warm. I looked underneath and I could see grey hairs sticking to the chassis," he said. "So I went back to headquarters and called the chief."

When the chief knocked at the mayor's door soon after, Edith MacLean said her husband was in bed asleep. The chief had the car seized, and investigation showed fresh blood and hair on the underneath of the car, as well as a half-finished bottle of brandy in the glove compartment. Certain of his facts now, Chief MacDonald had the mayor roused; MacLean had been drinking, but he was alert enough to ask if they'd found the bottle of brandy in the glove compartment. He was moaning and complaining of pain in his shoulder. MacDonald had him taken to St. Rita's Hospital, where he was charged and a constable was assigned to guard him.

Dr. Harold Devereux examined MacLean that night, finding a dislocated shoulder, a bruise on the left temple and a cut on his hand. He could have received the injuries from a fall or from a blow administered by a blunt instrument, the doctor said. MacLean refused to give a blood sample.

The city was bowled over by the news next day; for weeks after it was the talking point, and people began remembering another side of the respectable church elder—the boozy rascal who was always in one scrape or another. John Campbell, for example, remembered being at an accident where several army trucks had overturned outside Sydney. Mayor MacLean had driven up, emerging from his car grasping a quart bottle of ale.

"Anyone hurt?" he enquired. "No? That's all right then, boys, the government will pay the damage," said the mayor, doing a little jig back to his car just to please the crowd.

Four days after MacKinnon's death, city council received a letter from MacLean, written from his cell: "In view of the unfortunate circumstances surrounding the death of my lifelong friend Joseph MacKinnon, I hereby tender my resignation as mayor of the City of Sydney." Deputy Mayor Tony Gallagher immediately began a shake-up of the discredited city administration.

Today in Sydney some feel that Crown counsel Donald Finlayson was a wee bit hasty in charging the mayor with murder, but given the nature of the Nova Scotia political machine and the rough way the game was played, murder, after all, was not such a surprising outcome.

For his defence, MacLean shrewdly hired Ross McKimmie, an up-and-coming lawyer who was to become president of the Canadian Bar Association and a leading figure in the Alberta legal profession in later life.

The court battle, fought in the courthouse right across the street from MacLean's big green house, had its pathetic moments. When, for example, MacKinnon's wife was asked to identify her late husband's crutch, she broke into tears. The most damaging evidence came from Mrs. Susan MacDonald, who lived right beside the King's Road laneway and who had been putting out the ashes that Sunday night when, she testified, she heard the sound of men's voices arguing. "I then heard a loud scream, 'My God, Jack. Let me live!' " she said.

But MacLean, who pleaded not guilty, painted that Sunday as a pleasurable interlude of shared friendship: they got to the cottage, he said, and he went to the garage, got some wood and lit a fire. He and Joe sat before the fire talking and drinking. They had drunk half the bottle of brandy as well as the bottle of rum they'd brought with them and they'd also had some beers.

No disputes? "No," MacLean replied. "When Mr. Mac-Kinnon and I go out we are both Gaelickers and we like to speak the mother tongue, and that is what we used to do." The last he remembered, Joe was singing a little Gaelic song, and he, Jack, had gone to lie down on the couch because he was sleepy. Police had found the empty rum bottle, the beer bottles and used glasses at the cottage, and noted that the cottage door had been locked and the lights put out.

MacLean testified that he could remember nothing further until his wife woke him up at home some time after midnight to tell him the police wanted to speak to him.

His medical condition? "My shoulder was out of place, and I had a large lump on the side of my head. My eye was discoloured, I had three cracked ribs and my hip was black." But he had no idea how it happened and the charge, he said, "was the greatest shock of my life."

Finlayson asked him to explain why MacKinnon's $15,000 life insurance policy had been made payable to

MacLean to guarantee a $500 mortgage the mayor had given Joe.

"He must have wanted to protect me," said the mayor.

"Did you know Mr. MacKinnon was probably going to lose his job [over the voting scandal]?" asked Finlayson.

"I never knew or heard anything of the sort," said the mayor, straight-faced. Curiously, that was the only men-·tion made in the trial of what most people would have considered the motive. As Ian MacNeil wrote discerningly, "It has been a strange trial, fought on circumstantial evidence, with no hint as to motive."

The reason for the silence, Vic Coffin suspects, is that the case had brought notoriety to Sydney, the Crown going easy on MacLean "because we didn't want to be portrayed as a sort of mini-Chicago."

McKimmie argued in his summation that if someone intended to commit murder he would choose a quiet, remote spot. "Who would murder a man by McQuarrie's store?" he asked. And if MacKinnon was dead drunk in the back of the car, how could they fight and argue?

Chief Justice J.L. Ilsley ruled out murder immediately because, he said, intent to kill had not been proved. But when the jury returned after nearly three hours' deliberation, its verdict was "guilty of manslaughter." The mayor, considerably slimmer than in his heyday, blanched as he gripped the rail.

"You were and had been for years chief magistrate of a fine city," said the judge. MacLean, standing erect, seemed hardly to hear, his eyes looking beyond through the window to the grand green house from which he'd ruled this town. "Respect for law and order and the desirability of setting a good example should have been your guide," the voice went on. "Your own story and your actions on that Sunday indicate that this was not the case. It is, I think you realize, a shocking story."

But the judge recognized that MacLean was reputed to be "a warm-hearted, generous man who has helped many people." The sentence: three years in Dorchester penitentiary.

"It hit him hard," said Sheriff Jim MacKillop, recalling that day thirty years ago when he drove MacLean to Dorchester. "I remember," he said, "what a hard thing it was to walk away and leave him there when you realized he'd been mayor of our city."

Sander Muggah, the court clerk who recorded the sentence that day, was an old friend of MacLean's. "He behaved in court like a real gentleman. He didn't throw his weight around," said Muggah, erect and still working in the courts long after retirement age.

In the penitentiary, he said, MacLean was given a job tending chickens on the prison farm. When the other prisoners found out who he was, they gave him a hard time. "A little bit before it all happened, he was caught for impaired driving. But he appealed and got his licence back. Worst thing that could have happened!" said Muggah.

He closed the large legal book in which he'd been writing. "But you know, I have always been convinced that MacLean never meant to do any harm to MacKinnon," he said. "He was not of a mean nature."

* * *

We would like to believe too that D. Jack MacLean was the kindly soul the judge thought him; we want to believe, as some of his friends do, that the two affectionate old buddies were driving home together when they stopped the car and got out, and that Jack's foot hit the gas pedal by mistake and that he became confused. It would be nice to think of MacLean as just an amiable old boozer who drove home without realizing what had happened.

We'd like to, but another, darker picture intrudes on this rosy portrait. We learn in Sydney of people who went to see the mayor with their problems and who came away shaking after seeing their first citizen fly into such a rage they feared he would have a heart attack.

We learn from a relation of MacLean's and from a veteran police officer that years before, when MacLean was still a fisherman in Gabarus, forty-eight kilometres from Sydney, a number of men were out in the boat one day when MacLean had a furious argument with one of them. The man later mysteriously disappeared overboard.

To find out about the man who emerged from the gates of Dorchester penitentiary after serving the full three years, I tracked down a slim, well-preserved little woman of eighty, living today in a rented room on the outskirts of Sydney—his widow Edith.

The sweet, unforgettable smell of coal fires was in the air as I walked up the steps and found her dressed as smartly as you'd expect a mayor's wife to be; she was sitting alone watching afternoon television. Her face came to life as she remembered her husband's days of prominence. "The streets were never as clean as when he was mayor," she said. "He was the instigator of our City Hospital—but he never got credit for it." Then, in spite of herself, the memory of the "accident" intruded. "He should only have been charged with drunk driving," she said with a flash of anger.

Of course, the mayor's job didn't help his drinking, she added. "Meeting the ships off Sydney and going to those big conventions—they were all just big booze-ups."

When she and her brother-in-law went to pick up MacLean from Dorchester in 1953, he wasn't the same man. "It finished him. The first Sunday he went to church, but he had to resign as an elder, and that hurt him an awful lot."

With his criminal record, he was not able to go back into the insurance business. He went back to fishing, but gave that up after he slipped and cracked some ribs.

The afternoon sun caught the lines on her face, and her voice became almost inaudible as she came to the hard part of her story. "He was more erratic after that," she said softly. "Then he got . . . nervous." She searched in vain for a better word. "Yes . . . nervous. And I had to put him in the Cape Breton Mental Hospital."

The room was silent. There was the sound of teacups rattling in the kitchen. "He didn't even recognize me. . . ." she faltered. "He was in there four years when he died. That will be twelve years in March.

"But you see," she said, leaning forward, "I had no choice." Her voice faded to a whisper and I had to bend forward to catch her words. "It was him or me. You see, I was afraid he would choke me to death in the night."

The Body in the River

Nearly 100 years ago, behind the wide windows of a pretty, Anne-of-Green-Gables-style house, a teenager stood and watched with mounting fear as men rowed up and down the broad South-West River, probing its depths with grapple hooks. Every morning when Will Millman got up they were there, rowing and probing. Then one day one of the men caught a glimpse of something gold flashing beneath the water; it was Mary Tuplin's long, fair hair, floating and waving in the current like seaweed.

By then Will Millman was gone. Fear pounding in his heart, the nineteen-year-old had caught the train to Charlottetown for the first time in his life and, awkward and uncomfortable in his farm clothes, he'd found his way to the office of lawyer E.J. Hodgson.

"They think I killed her," he said, unburdening himself to the attorney. "Her father's going around saying he's going to take out a warrant against me. And I didn't touch her, honest, I didn't touch her. You've got to stop them, Mr. Hodgson. Can't we sue him for slander or something?" Hodgson calmed the boy and sent him home, advising him to ignore the rumours until the matter of Mary Tuplin's disappearance sorted itself out.

But when young Millman, a plain, straight-looking fellow with a lick of hair across his forehead, got home that July evening in 1887 he knew his ordeal was just beginning: some 100 carts and carriages blocked the road in front of the Millman farm, and in the field beyond a few hundred people crowded around as the coroner began his inquest into the death of sixteen-year-old Mary Pickering Tuplin.

On the nearby bank, in the red glow of the setting sun, lay the body of Mary Tuplin in a cotton pinafore and dress and boots, two bullets lodged in her head, her stomach already swelling with a six-month foetus. Beside her lay the forty-five kilogram (100-pound) sandstone rock to which her body had been roped.

The storybook province of Prince Edward Island in the late 1800s, complete with its pretty farms and a narrow-minded, meeting-going population, was splintered by the Millman–Tuplin murder case. Many Islanders were roused to demand the lynching of young William; young women were equally roused to pray and weep for his vindication.

"If it had happened to people of no account it would have soon been forgotten," ruminated William Johnstone, a member of the Tuplin family who in his earlier days knew Will Millman's brother Bradford well. "But it didn't. The Millmans and the Tuplins were well-to-do and highly regarded families, and the countryside around here is still full of Millmans and Tuplins."

Out near Margate, the Millman family home sits incongruously today in the middle of Woodleigh Replicas, a tourist showplace of miniature British monuments built in stone; York Minster Cathedral towers in tiny defiance in the front yard, and the Tower of London now rules where the Millmans used to corral their cows.

But walking through the large house that once sheltered the Millmans and their many children, the days of a century ago come alive again. With what feelings of shame and anger must William have gazed from the upstairs window across the river at the Tuplin farm! And when the word broke, what prayers and tears must his parents have offered up in the large kitchen where, for a while after, Mrs. Millman lost her wits.

Will and Mary's relationship had begun casually—a dance at Francis Hillman's on New Year's Eve 1886. Admission was twenty-five cents, and all the farm girls and boys were flushed and perspiring as they jigged to the tunes of the fiddlers. If Will had met Mary before, he'd only regarded her offhandedly, but under the spell of the dancing and the odd drop of whisky gulped slyly behind the barn, he saw her now, with her warm cheeks and flashing eyes, as a desirable girl.

At 3:00 in the morning, with his friend Francis Power following behind, he walked Mary home, going with her into the darkened farmhouse for half an hour. Whatever the outcome of the fumbling and giggling in front of the wood stove, Will agreed to come and see her again the following week. When he arrived at the Tuplin house the evening of January 5, Mary's parents and many brothers and sisters were there, but finally everyone went to bed, and the young couple had the kitchen to themselves.

John Tuplin was to remember waking at approximately 3:00 A.M. and, not seeing Mary in her bed, calling to her downstairs. He heard the discreet sound of the back door closing, and Mary came upstairs to bed right away.

Strangely, Millman had no further dealings with Mary Tuplin. If, as he told his friend Power, he had had intercourse with her that night, it's surprising Millman did not become a frequent late-night guest in the Tuplin kitchen. Will Millman, of course, could have felt remorse. His family was fervently religious—the Millmans had named one of their sons after the local minister; Mrs. Millman had had a mental lapse when, in her fervour, she visualized heaven as fortified by a brass shield against which her prayers bounced in vain.

In any event, Will Millman was soon found courting

another young woman of good family, and it must have come as a rough surprise to him when he heard rumours that Mary was carrying his child. Attending church on Sunday, June 26, he approached Tom Bryenton, the sexton, and a friend of the Tuplins.

"Is it true Mary Tuplin's having a baby?" he asked.

"Well, I've heard talk," replied Bryenton.

"And she's saying it's mine?"

Bryenton nodded. "I'd like to see her to ask her about it," Will said at last. "But I'm kind of ashamed to go up there." Bryenton said he and his wife were going that evening to see the Tuplins' little boy who was seriously ill, and he'd ask Mary on the quiet to come outside the farmhouse to talk to Will.

John Tuplin, a farmer and hard-headed proprietor of the nearby Black Horse Inn, cast a suspicious eye on Bryenton when the sexton asked Mary that evening to step outside for a word with his wife. Mary went, and shortly after she had a talk with Will Millman on the road near the farm, the outcome of which is not known. But the Tuplins had other worries beside their daughter's condition: their little boy died in the next hours, and two days later they made their unhappy way to the cemetery to bury him.

They arrived home from the funeral between 5:00 and 6:00 P.M. and had a glum tea. Mary, wearing a thin cotton dress and old boots, went out and milked the cows and later played inside with one of her sister's small children. At dusk, just before the lamps were lit, somewhere between 8:00 and 9:00 P.M., she handed the child back to her sister, got up and went out without a word. She never returned.

Time is a crucial element in deciding if Will Millman was waiting in the shadows outside to take her down a lane called the Mud Road that night. Between 6:00 and 7:00, a schoolgirl, Dorothy Adams, crossing her father's potato field near the Mud Road to get the cows in for milking, saw someone tying up a boat. "It was William Millman," she was to declare with certainty, although she was about sixty-five metres from the river at the time. Her father, Jonathan Adams, was weeding his garden that evening and had noticed the boat tied up near his property about 7:00 P.M.

The same time or a little earlier, young Donald Tuplin, perhaps wanting to escape the gloomy atmosphere at home, went with some other boys to fetch Churchill Underhill's cow. As they came to a turn in the Mud Road, they saw a startling sight: a man sitting beside the road with his elbows on his knees, covering his face with undergrowth to conceal his identity. "I thought it was an old crazy man," he said, and the boys had run back up the road in fear. A Tuplin son-in-law, James Somers, also saw the strange figure, his face covered with undergrowth and wearing a brown straw hat, on the Mud Road, and although he had never seen Millman before, he was to swear in court, "He [Millman] is the same man I saw sitting at the end of the Mud Road."

George Profit, who lived at the Black Horse Inn, remembered John Tuplin coming in about 9:30 that night looking for Mary. After Tuplin left, Profit was in the house cutting George Clarke's hair when he heard two shots from the direction of the river. John Sudsbury, waiting outside the Irishtown Church "to take home my missus from the meeting," also heard the two shots shortly before the meeting ended.

Driving home from a lecture, Andrew Woodside had heard a shot and a scream. He had whipped his horse into a gallop at that moment, and did not hear a second shot. The time: between 9:50 and 10:20 P.M.

Earlier that evening Mrs. Millman had suggested to her husband that they go to the church meeting, which had been called to discuss a picnic.

"It's too late," said John Millman. "What's the time now?"

"It's only twenty to seven. You can make it if you hurry," said their daughter Mary Eliza, and everyone in the family remembered her words. The Millmans rushed to wash and change their clothes, and John harnessed the horses to the wagon. It was 7:00 when they left, and everyone remembered that William was still at home, although he said he was going down to the river for a swim.

The Reverend Thomas Reagh, a bit of a stickler for time, was to calculate that the meeting that night ended at exactly 10:00 P.M.; he got home at 10:15. That's important, because when the Millmans got home at or just before 10:30 P.M., William was just going to bed.

"Good night, Da," he said, as he went upstairs.

John Tuplin, meanwhile, had been going from one house to another looking for Mary, stopping to shout a loud "Hallo Mary," across the still, moonlit fields. Finally he went to bed, but got up at daybreak to resume the search.

A handkerchief with the initial "M" embroidered in the corner was eventually found on the riverbank and identified as Mary's, and John Cousins on the following Friday found his oyster boat, which had been padlocked on the Millman bank of the South-West River, with its lock broken, the forty-five kilogram rock he kept in her for ballast missing. The same day a group of men began dragging the river.

Six days after she had walked from the family kitchen, Mary Tuplin's body was found beneath one metre of water. Her body showed no sign of violence—except for a small, inconspicuous wound just above one ear where postmortem doctors found a bullet, flat as a button, which had struck the thick part of the skull. That bullet should only have stunned her; opening the cranium they found a second slug which had penetrated the brain, killing her instantly.

When the carriages and crowds finally left, Will Millman slept little. At dawn the next morning he heard voices downstairs, and Constable Alexander McKay came up to tell him to get dressed—he was under arrest. In country fashion, the constable ate an awkward breakfast with the Millmans before setting off to drive his prisoner to town. John Tuplin, remembering Tom Bryenton's whispered aside to his daughter the Sunday before her murder, also had the sexton arrested as an accomplice, although he was released soon afterwards.

The impact of the murder was being felt far from the little villages most concerned. "MARGATE HORROR. MURDER MOST FOUL," the Charlottetown *Examiner* screamed. On July 8 angry crowds milled around the railway station in Charlottetown to glimpse Millman on his way to jail. Police, hoping to avoid them, drove him into town in a carriage. But on the outskirts of town he was spotted by men who turned and sped back to spread the news that Millman was coming. By the time the carriage approached the jail, the crowd which had gathered there was so large it had to drive right past. "Lynch him!" some shouted. "Hang him!" Soldiers finally had to clear a way into the jail for the pale, frightened youth.

With the province in an uproar over the murder, Premier W.W. Sullivan, who also acted as attorney-general, saw political mileage in prosecuting the Millman case personally. This added ferment to the excitement when at last, on January 12, 1888, Millman was driven from prison in a sleigh and led into court. It was getting dark in the afternoon as he entered the courtroom. The gas lights had not yet been lit, but those on the packed benches could see a slight, erect figure with a ruddy face and dark hair. The crowd had come prepared to see a brute, but as some left that evening a reporter heard the remarks, "He has a nice face, hasn't he now?" and "He's not such a bad-looking fellow, is he?"

The Crown had prepared its case well: Constable McKay had found two right foot marks in the hardened mud on the edge of the river early in the investigation, the smaller one matching Mary's boot, the larger one belonging to a man. He had also seized a pistol which William Millman had borrowed from Francis Power, wanting to try it out before deciding whether to buy it. When Will returned the firearm to Power after Mary disappeared, two of the five bullets had been fired.

Most damaging of all, Francis Power's sixteen-year-old

brother Patrick testified that two days after Mary Tuplin disappeared, Millman had asked him if he would swear that he had been with him the night of June 28th at Paynter's Line, in the opposite direction to the Tuplin farm. At first Power agreed, and had proceeded to swear out an affidavit to that effect before he changed his mind.

Defence lawyer Hodgson argued that Millman had been foolish to try to get Power to lie for him, but that this had been done to save his mother's sanity, for which he feared. Hodgson also called a Charlottetown ammunition dealer who showed the bullets that had entered Mary Tuplin's body were of a different brand than those found in Power's gun, and other witnesses testified that Millman had fired off the two bullets in their presence, one at the side of the road and another into a plank of wood. The tide seemed to be turning for Millman when the meticulous Constable McKay, recalled to the stand, carefully measured Millman's boots and shoes in the witness box and found them considerably larger than the prints he'd found and measured by the river.

In his summation, Hodgson argued powerfully that Millman was still at home when he was reported seen in the boat, and that given the time the shots were heard, William could not possibly have had time to put the body in the boat, pole it half a kilometre, dump the body, then make his way three-quarters of a kilometre to greet his parents arriving home from church. Repeatedly he told the jury, "We aren't here to ascertain who murdered Mary Tuplin, but to find whether or not the prisoner at the bar did so."

But if not Millman, then who? The potent feelings at the time of the trial indicate that if Millman had not been found guilty, life in close-knit, respectable Margate would have become uncomfortable with everyone under suspicion.

Justice William Hensley, in his summation, made it clear that in his view Millman had had enough time to commit the crime and return home.

It was 7:30 P.M. on the eleventh day of the trial when the jury returned following three hours of deliberation. Millman was led in looking flushed and feverish and holding a handkerchief to his face. As he heard the word "guilty," he looked dazed, then collapsed. The courtroom was cleared, and fifteen minutes later Millman was taken to his cell to await his sentence.

The *Daily Examiner* stormed: "Two young lives have been lost to the world, two respectable families have been forced to endure misery unutterable, the good name of two flourishing settlements has been seriously compromised and, indeed, the whole province has suffered on account of the awful crime committed on the South-West River on the 28th of June last."

But from the heights of its Victorian sanctimony, the *Examiner* could find but one grievous flaw on which to blame this moral catastrophe—the disturbing trend towards "courting at night."

"It is a common thing for a young man to go to a farm-house in the evening and for the family to retire, leaving him and a woman to sit up alone, hugging and kissing and talking nonsense or worse until daylight," the paper wrote, "unduly exciting their nerves, losing their sleep, indulging in improper thoughts, rendering very difficult the preservation of purity and the innocence of youth. . . .

"The sin of impurity brought down upon Sodom and Gommorah a terrible punishment, and it will be well for Prince Edward Island if the lesson taught by the murder of Mary Tuplin and the fate of William Millman is heeded. If it is not heeded, a worse thing may befall us."

Eleven of the jurors petitioned for mercy for the boy, and sympathetic jailers kept him in a large airy room rather than locked in the condemned cell. Appeals were made, but on March 27 Hodgson informed William Millman that his final appeal to commute the death sentence had been denied.

As chief jailer Harvie brought him a basket of provisions sent by a well-wisher, Millman hit him over the head with a bottle and stunned him. Harvie recovered and tried to grapple with him, but Millman dodged out into the prison yard.

There he was recaptured and was locked in the death cell with a leg iron.

On April 10 large crowds, including many young women who wept openly, gathered in front of the jail for the hanging. When the hangman came to his cell to bind him just before 8:00 A.M., Millman took one last greedy look through the barred window at the blue sky, then allowed the bandages to be placed over his eyes.

He walked out calmly, his lips moving as he prayed, and was guided up the steps to the three-metre-high platform. Twelve and a half minutes after the hangman touched the lever, his heart stopped beating; he was laid in a plain pine coffin and taken for burial to the People's Cemetery. On the coffin's lid a plaque said simply: "William Millman, Jesu Mercy."

In his last hours Millman had entrusted a letter to the mayor of Charlottetown for publication after his death:

> At my trial there was false swearing and false evidence against me and because of this I was found guilty and they have taken my life. It was hard at first to forgive them, but I do forgive them; God knows I do and I pray for them. When I tried to escape I did not mean to hurt Mr. Harvie; it was only to escape I did what I done. I have no fear of dying, but I don't say that boasting. One thing I want to say—I had the best father and mother a boy ever had. One of these days all will be known. Oh, my God, I do look forward to that day.

* * *

Bowling along the highway past the prosperous farms that show no sign that the Lord has brought down the punishment of Sodom and Gommorah on the heads of Islanders, Millman's words stick in my mind: "One of these days all will be known. . . ."

Some five kilometres up the road from the murder scene I find William Johnstone, frail now and one of the few

Islanders who remembers some of the principals in the case.

"Yes," he says looking over his glasses, "There are still a lot of strong feelings over it."

Was Millman guilty? Johnstone's answer is a long time coming. "There was an uncle of Millman's," he says at last. "Right afterwards he went away to California and never came back. A lot of people believe he was involved."

That's probably as near as we'll ever come to solving the Millman–Tuplin mystery.

The Case of the Missing Baby

It's snowing heavily this January afternoon as I drive along the narrow, tree-lined back road—as it was that January day in 1936 when the two Bannister boys and their sister trudged ten kilometres to Pacific Junction through knee-high snow to get the baby.

I stop the car near the clearing where the Lake family's shack once stood and where Bertha Lake's naked body was found lying in the road, a deep gash in her forehead. And over there, twelve metres away and partly covered by the drifting snow, they found her twenty-month-old boy Jackie, unmarked, but frozen after he had crawled out of his dead mother's arms trying to find his way back to the warmth.

The snow wraps the New Brunswick woods in silence; overhead, bare branches touch and clasp across the road, and in the growing darkness I feel the presence of May Bannister who, though dead these ten years, still commands a shiver of respect in these parts.

Bosomy and blowsy, course-tongued, crude, she was capable of anything—blackmail, kidnapping, perhaps even murder. She concocted one of the most bizarre schemes in the annals of Canadian wrongdoing; when her scheme backfired it led to the execution of her two sons.

Yet, given the mean circumstances of her life, there is a certain magnificence to May Bannister: she was a pauper living on Salvation Army handouts, yet she could dress like a duchess. She met adversity brazenly, and she went to her grave laughing. Studying the defiant, almost masculine features of her "official" portrait taken in jail by a *New York Daily News* photographer, one wonders about other May Bannisters that there might be in the world, saved from her fate only because of kinder circumstances.

The era had much to do with the Bannister crime. It took place during the depths of the Depression, a time when many of the people living in this poor section of countryside twenty kilometres from Moncton were forced onto scrubby little farms by the lack of jobs and opportunities elsewhere. May Bannister, her slow-witted sons, twenty-year-old Daniel and eighteen-year-old Arthur, and their younger sisters Frances, aged fifteen, and Marie, aged thirteen, had moved into a broken-down house in Berry's Mill where May kept them clothed and fed on charity handouts and the occasional generosity of men friends lured into her substantial arms.

* * *

Pacific Junction was the name given to a collection of shacks marking an important railway junction. It was there that Philip Lake, after losing his job as a Marconi wireless rigger, had found the abandoned pig farm to which he had brought his common-law wife Bertha and their little son Jackie. They did the best they could: Phil, an easygoing six-footer and a good worker, got occasional jobs on the highways; but they depended primarily on their cow, their eighteen chickens and the pig for survival. For all their meagre means, the Lakes kept an open door for strangers in their two-room shack built from old boxcar timbers.

The Bannister youngsters were drawn to the Lakes, often walking the long road to Pacific Junction for a meal or a talk. After Bertha had a baby, Elizabeth Ann ("Betty"), in

August, the Bannisters increased their visits. And in the fall of 1935, they asked the Lakes a strange question: could they have little Betty to bring up at home? The Lakes laughed off the request, and put it down to the Bannisters' naivety.

On New Year's Eve another young friend of the Lakes', Earl O'Brien, happened by on a rabbit-snaring trip in the woods. "Come on in, boy. Get warm by the stove," said Lake, his ready smile revealing the only objects of value in their pasteboard and newspaper-lined home—his two shining gold teeth. O'Brien, who had stayed with the Lakes the previous summer for a few days, had brought Jackie a toy car as a belated Christmas present, and he stayed to celebrate a quiet New Year with them.

With the new baby it was a bit crowded in the cabin, so on New Year's Day, O'Brien, who still hadn't caught any rabbits, asked if they'd mind if he moved the chickens into the barn and cleaned out the henhouse to make himself a little "camp" for the night. Phil helped him move the chickens, and O'Brien washed the floor with scalding water, spending the day improvising a stove with a steel drum.

That evening another friend, Otto Blakney, who had camped on the Lakes' place the previous summer while building himself a cabin in the woods, came by for supper too, and afterwards Bertha proudly brought out five-month-old Betty for him to admire. As a bachelor, Blakney said he "wasn't one for babies," but even he became attentive as Bertha parted the child's thick, dark hair to show him an unusual strawberry birthmark on Betty's head. "Birthmarks run in my family," she said.

There was a knock at the door, and Arthur Bannister came in, stamping off the snow and standing his .22 rifle by the door. He too had been laying rabbit snares, and when he heard O'Brien was staying the night in the henhouse, asked if he too could stay so that he could check his snares in the morning. O'Brien sat up all night, keeping the fire going, and soon after midnight he heard a door slam and someone call, "Arthur." Bannister went out, and O'Brien heard voices and caught a glimpse of a teenage boy and girl. After about twenty minutes, Arthur returned.

"It was my brother and sister," he said. "They want me to go home. But I ain't going. I want to check my snares in the morning." O'Brien little realized that he had just witnessed a dress rehearsal for a crime; had it not been for his presence, the Bannisters might have carried out their scheme that night.

On Sunday, January 5, there was a snowstorm. But at about 2:00 P.M., Arthur, ignoring the storm, left home carrying his rifle on his back. Leaving the road, where he was more likely to be seen, he followed the main CNR railway track to Pacific Junction, but his attempt to avoid detection failed when Len Carroll, out walking his dog along the track, heard the animal barking up ahead. A figure loomed out of the snow. "Oh, I see who you are," said Carroll, recognizing Arthur, and they stopped and chatted for a few moments.

Railway section man William Horseman also remembered looking out of his window near the tracks that afternoon and seeing one of the Bannister boys walking along with a gun on his back. At 8:00 P.M., just as the storm was letting up, Daniel and Frances Bannister also left home and laboured through the deep snow, arriving at the Lakes' cabin around midnight.

Shortly after that Omar Lutes, the CNR station agent at Pacific Junction, and his wife were awakened when their six-month-old Alsatian dog began barking furiously. Mrs. Lutes got up, looked out the window for a while, then called the dog in. Stubbornly the dog kept barking and running back and forth towards the road. "Aw, be quiet," she said finally, and went back to bed.

The next morning Otto Blakney went into the woods to cut firewood; about 11:00 A.M. he was walking down the road towards the Lake place when he saw smoke up ahead. He ran into the clearing—and could see only glowing ashes where the cabin had stood. As he turned to go to the station for help, he noticed several sets of tracks leading away from the house and along the road.

By the side of the road, he spotted a baby's bottle, the milk inside frozen hard, then he noticed bloodstains in the snow. He came first to little Jackie, who was wearing a brown coat and diaper, lying face-down and frozen. A little further on he found Bertha lying on her back, her hands clasped across her breasts, naked except for a strip of cloth around her waist. The snow around her was flattened and bloodstained as though by a struggle or by the thrashing of her body. The footprints continued a few metres, then branched off the road.

At the station Blakney told Lutes the news, then phoned the police. Months later in the witness box Omar Lutes could not describe what he saw that morning without his voice breaking. The two men went back to the murder scene, observed the deep gash that had fractured Bertha's skull, then went to look at the smouldering remains of the house.

Picking their way through the contorted lumps of metal and molten glass, they found the blackened mass of a body, its grey bones protruding. The legs had been burned off above the knees and the arms above the elbows.

Lutes leaned over the charred body, still hot to the touch. "It's Phil, look," he said, and there, shining in the upper jaw, were the two gold teeth. Royal Canadian Mounted Police who arrived soon afterwards on a rail car concluded that baby Betty's body had been totally consumed in the fire; the only other bones they found were those of a cat.

The footprints in the snow, a long, bayonetlike knife plunged into a snow bank, a man's muleskin mitten found near the ruins of the house and the fatal wound in Bertha's head soon convinced the RCMP that they were dealing with murder.

Shortly afterwards, coroner Dr. Robert J. Caldwell arrived on the train. Caldwell had no difficulty recognizing the woman's frozen body: he had delivered Bertha's baby. He ordered the bodies transported back to the station by toboggan. In Moncton x-rays were eventually to reveal a bullet lodged in Phil Lake's brain, the likely cause of his death.

Snow, so often the policeman's friend in tracking criminals in the harsh Canadian climate, soon told its story. The police were able to follow Bertha's pathetic course as she stumbled and fell five times before dying. They followed the tracks of the three Bannisters, observing where they had stopped to rest on their long trek home and where one had dragged what might have been a gun.

Lee Johnson, a farmer who carted produce and firewood in to Moncton from Berry's Mill, had been out early that morning and, he told police, he'd noticed the group of tracks in the fresh snow leading from the direction of Pacific Junction and turning off at the Bannisters. By the first evening of their investigation, the Mounties were knocking at the Bannisters' door.

Yes, agreed Daniel Bannister, the muleskin mitten belonged to him, but Arthur had borrowed the mittens from him. "I don't even know where Pacific Junction is," he claimed. The knife, too, was his. The Mounties took Arthur to Moncton and charged him with murder, theorizing that the tragedy occurred after a drinking party when, perhaps, Arthur had made sexual advances to Bertha, and Lake and he had argued.

A couple of days later Daniel was also arrested, and Frances was detained as a material witness. But the police still considered the affair just another drunken brawl and seemed satisfied with Arthur's statement that Lake, after a few drinks, had made indecent advances to his sister Frances. A fight followed and Lake threw a log which, Arthur claimed, struck Bertha in the forehead. Arthur hit Phil over the head, knocking him out, but an oil lamp was knocked over, setting the shack ablaze, and the Bannisters fled.

The truth emerged by the merest chance. On Thursday, police matron Maude LeBlanc and RCMP Constable Gale Swaney went to the Bannister home to pick up a pair of slacks for Frances, who was still in jail. "The Mounted Police are a damned bunch of murderers," May snarled at them. "They promised to bring the children [Arthur, Daniel and Frances] home, that's what liars they are."

While Mrs. Bannister, still muttering, went upstairs to look for a pair of slacks for Frances, Constable Swaney sat down with Milton Trites, a second-hand store owner and neighbour who often helped out the Bannisters with food and small amounts of money. He had just been reading a newspaper account of the arrest of Arthur and Daniel to May and her daughter Marie, neither of whom could read, when the police had arrived.

"Yeh," said Trites, "Sure is tough on May, what with her boys being locked up and her having the baby to look after."

"Baby. What baby?" snapped Mrs. LeBlanc.

"Well, May's little baby girl. She just brought it home," replied Trites. Mrs. LeBlanc tried to search the house on the pretext of finding another pair of slacks for Frances, but May Bannister, visibly nervous, barred her way in front of a bedroom door like a cornered tiger.

"I'll be back," Mrs. LeBlanc told her.

The next evening she returned with Moncton City Police Inspector H.V. Harris and insisted on seeing the whole house. Sure enough, in May Bannister's bedroom they found an undernourished baby wearing brand-new baby clothes. The helpful Milton Trites was left in charge of the baby while Mrs. Bannister, telling different stories, was taken to Moncton for questioning.

"Ask Mrs. Cool at the Travellers' Aid, she knows it's my baby," she claimed. Mrs. Cool demurred.

"Talk to the people at the Windsor Hotel. I checked in there with the baby last Saturday," she pleaded. The Windsor Hotel hadn't heard of her.

"Milton knows it's mine. He saw me with the baby before ever the tragedy happened at Pacific Junction." Milton remembered seeing the baby for the first time Monday afternoon.

"Look," Mrs. LeBlanc told her, "I'll bring a doctor to

examine you. That'll settle whether it's your baby."

"No goddamn doctor is going to examine me!" snapped May, and that was that.

Leaving May pacing up and down the police station, by turns storming and sobbing, the police went back to the house at 2:00 A.M., wrapped up little Betty, brought her to Moncton on a sleigh, and had her admitted to hospital. May Bannister, now charged with kidnapping, joined her two sons who, for their own safety, had been lodged comfortably in the women's cells ("I could get to like it here—if only I was free to come and go," one of them told the jailer).

In the following days the outline of May Bannister's plot began to emerge. It was not maternal instinct that had prompted her to welcome the little baby so warmly when Daniel had walked in with her in his arms at 3:00 A.M. the previous Monday: little Betty was to be a meal ticket.

It turned out that the hapless Milton Trites had employed Mrs. Bannister as a part-time housekeeper for $2 a week, extra overnight duties included in the price. Milton no doubt thought he was getting a bargain until Mrs. Bannister, forty-three at the time, informed him she was expecting his child.

She was always a big woman, so it was hard for Milton to tell if she was telling the truth. May informed him November 1 that she was going to a friend's to have the baby. He received a few letters postmarked Moncton, no doubt written for her, informing him that the little baby girl weighed nine pounds and that her name was Thyra. He didn't see May again until December 29, although she had, without his knowing, been home a number of times.

May's plan was to force Milton to pay child support, but there was only one problem: she needed a baby. The plot had been afoot a long time; the previous February she had had Frances write a letter for her to the protestant orphanage in Saint John. It said: "Dear Secretary, I find your ad in the paper, Homes for Babies. I will give a baby a home under six months old. My choice would be a girl."

On Christmas Eve, May had bought a life-size doll in the

Metropolitan store in Moncton, ostensibly a Christmas present for Marie. Oddly enough, she was seen walking about town with it wrapped in a blanket like a real baby. "Want to see my baby?" May would ask men friends, then whisk it away before they could see it was only a doll.

May had a second reason for desperately wanting the Lake baby: for months she had been setting a trap for another man, a God-fearing do-gooder by the name of Albert Powell who befriended the Bannisters and held Sunday School classes and prayer meetings in their home. Far from deriving spiritual comfort from these ministrations, May accused poor Powell of seducing thirteen-year-old Marie, and said if he didn't pay support for the baby Marie was expecting she'd shoot him. Obviously little Betty was to be in the unique position of having two mothers and two fathers, with both men eager to pay for her modest needs.

In the witness stand, Powell, a CNR employee, was to declare, "I am innocent. I am an innocent man." Few would argue with him.

Police matron LeBlanc told friends that May just plain scared her. And in the witness box she laughed when it was suggested that she had tried to bully May into signing a confession. "You can't scare her!" she said.

But, oh, how she could weep. May wept for the cameraman when she embraced her poor boys in jail. She sobbed every time Frances had to get up again and tell how she'd gone that night to the Lakes' "to get the baby," and she cried a storm throughout her own trial.

We will never know whether the instructions May Bannister issued to her simple-minded sons included murder. Whether through fear or mute loyalty, none of her children would speak of her role: Frances and Marie hung their heads any time they were asked in the witness box about their mother's involvement, and the two boys never testified. But it's difficult to believe that with the scheme planned days before (and aborted once), and with Arthur carrying a gun, the possibility of violence had not been foreseen. For how else would they get the baby? And in that house of dull-witted, apathetic youngsters, there was only one person with the cunning to conceive such a scheme: May Bannister.

The most Frances would admit to was Arthur coming out of the Lake cabin as she arrived and handing her the baby wrapped in a blanket. As she started for home, she heard the sound of a shot, and soon after the two boys caught up with her. She had seen fire behind them and heard a woman screaming, but they hadn't turned back.

One of the brothers, she wasn't sure which, had broken Arthur's rifle in two on a fence and thrown the pieces away. The barrel and stock were later found by police after ten men had sifted through the snow for days in the area where they suspected the gun had been thrown. Their diligence was rewarded; a ballistics expert testified that the bullet found in Lake's head had been fired from Arthur's .22.

For the crowds that filled the public benches in the Bannister trials, the high point was always the appearance of baby Betty. Whether placidly taking her bottle in the arms of a Mountie, whose face was as red as his tunic, or fretting while policemen and lawyers argued over her identity (the strawberry birthmark determined the outcome), the baby always won their hearts. (She was, I heard, adopted by Bertha Lake's sister in Fredericton, and was left to a blessed obscurity.)

Arthur and Daniel seemed hardly to realize the seriousness of their position, grinning and sometimes laughing at the grisly evidence of their crime. The defence counsel, T. Murray Lambert, argued that since the Crown had failed to establish which of the brothers committed the crime, the jury was being asked to speculate.

But both were found guilty and, with tears in his eyes, Chief Justice J.H. Barry sentenced them to death. But he had no regrets as he turned to May Bannister, who had been found not guilty of the more serious charges and had been convicted only of harbouring a stolen child.

"Mrs. Bannister, stand up!" he said with loathing. He could not understand why the jury had let her off so lightly, he said, as he gave her the maximum three-and-a-half-year sentence.

Arthur won a short reprieve when his conviction was overturned on appeal, but a second jury was quick to find him guilty, and on September 23, 1936, the two brothers walked to the gallows in the women's section of the county jail in Dorchester.

"The rope's too tight. I can't say my prayers," said Arthur as the hangman adjusted the noose. They were his last words.

May served her time in Kingston women's penitentiary, then came bouncing back to Berry's Mill as if nothing had happened. "I was terrified of her," Bessie Horsman, a local farmer's wife, told me. "We'd see her walking into town when we were driving in and my husband would say, 'Why don't we pick her up?' I'd say, 'If that woman gets in this car, I get out.'

"And then, wouldn't you know it, I ended up in hospital in the same room as her! And she was just as nice as can be to me. She called me 'dear' all the time. She had no time for religion, I remember. When the minister would come round, she'd get rid of him real quick.

" 'I don't need no prayers,' she'd tell him. 'Just bury me deep enough so the birds don't peck my eyes out!' Then she'd give a great big laugh."

Mrs. Horsman couldn't help laughing. "And if there was anything she didn't like on the menu, she told the doctor right quick—and they had to bring her the best there was in the hospital.

"That was a terrible thing she did, and her boys hanged for it. She was capable of anything. Yet she walked into Moncton pretty near every day to get things for her kids and her grandchildren when they came. She always kept them dressed pretty good, too," she said with grudging admiration.

Ernie Little, who used to keep the store at Berry's Mill, remembered walking in one day and finding Marie ill with consumption, and no food in the house for the children. "It was bad. I phoned the overseer of the poor, and from that day until she died May was on welfare," he said. Often, he said, he would pick her up on the road as she walked from Moncton with a bag of bread she'd been given. "Of course," he added, in case I thought he was sympathizing with her, "she should have hanged instead of those boys."

"I often used to pick those two boys up on my way to town," Lee Johnson, the man who followed the tracks in the snow so long ago, told me. "They was always going into Moncton begging for day-old bread and the like. I don't know that you'd say they was mentally deficient. But they had no education. They were simple, and I thought they were harmless enough.

"Now their mother, that was different. She was to blame. You know," he said as we finished our talk about May, "there's no animal on earth as peculiar as a human being."

Good-bye, Olive Swimm, and Sleep

Crouched behind the barn he could see the smoke coming from the chimney and now and again the glimpse of a light flowered dress as the woman passed in front of the window. The snow was thick on the ground, and he shivered as he waited, pulling the light grey raincoat tighter around him.

The sun had gone and his hands were growing numb when finally the door to the summer kitchen opened and a heftily built man with dark hair emerged carrying an axe. He shrank back against the wall, his icy fingers gripping the revolver with the broken spring. "God, let it work," he prayed as the sharp thud of the axe splitting the logs echoed back from the woods. "God, let it work." The man finished splitting, gathered up an armful of wood and was carrying it back to the farmhouse when Benny Swimm stepped in front of him, the faulty gun in his hand.

There are murder cases that, like lightning over a shipwreck, split the sky and illuminate the human condition. Such was the Benny Swimm case. It was motivated by the oldest of human passions, sex and jealousy, and it reminds us that in the backwoods of New Brunswick in the 1920s, and for decades after, Canada had its own hillbillies—poor, downtrodden people living on the proceeds of moonshine and the game they could shoot, their lives marred by violence and incest.

The story of Benny Swimm's lust and revenge has all the brooding inevitability of one of William Faulkner's epics of rural violence in the Deep South. And the final scene, related to me by an elderly lawyer who was there that day at the Carleton County Jail in Woodstock, was so gruesome that he still finds it hard to talk about sixty years later.

The story has its beginnings at the turn of the century when Benny was born in a one-room shack in the New Brunswick "badlands"—the poor, borderline farmland that edges thousands of square kilometres of impenetrable forest on the east side of the Saint John River, north of Woodstock. Benny, a moody, difficult boy, didn't get along at home and went to live with his Uncle John in the woods at the back of Hartland. He adapted no better at school. One day when he was twelve he came home glowering. "How can I stop those kids at school plaguing the life outta me?" he asked his uncle.

"Rip their bloody guts out," said John Swimm shortly. Benny took him to heart. After school the next day when the taunting began, he ran at a crowd of students, slashing and swinging with his knife. He never returned to school.

As he grew into lonely manhood, there was one consoling feature in Benny's drab existence: his uncle's daughter, Olive Swimm, a bright, attractive girl. We are fortunate in having a picture of the Swimm household and of conditions in the badlands during that period from an English policeman and writer, William Guy Carr, who set down his memories some years after the murder case.

Coming to New Brunswick after serving in World War I, Carr was shocked to find what he described as "the poorest human beings I have ever met in a civilized country." His work as a policeman brought him in daily contact with the moonshiners, and he recalled standing on a hill within sight of the shacks of six families, only one of which could say that its members had not in the past few years been charged with murder or incest.

Children commonly told him that, sleeping in the same room with their parents and older brothers and sisters, they would play at "mothers and fathers" from the age of six on. Carr had only pity for these poor people who had been steadily pushed to the edge of the wilderness. Many were the times, he wrote, that he saw them coming to town with their eggs, butter or chickens to sell.

"How much are eggs today?" the farmer would ask the storekeeper.

"Ain't buying none . . . got more'n I know how to sell," the merchant would tell him glumly. After trying to sell his produce all over town, the farmer would finally come back and ask how much he could get in trade for his produce. Scratching his head, the storekeeper would say, "Well, seeing it's you, I'll give you fifteen cents a dozen." The result, wrote Carr, was that the farmers had to sell their produce at drastically deflated prices, receiving goods for which they were paying premium prices in exchange. In addition, as they steadily sank into debt their creditors would insist they sell the produce of their farms to them at giveaway prices.

These conditions produced an embittered people, forever on the point of eviction, who were forced to make what they could from hunting or from the illegal liquor trade. The badlands had become rough, dangerous country where men lived by their guns and where lawmen had been known to disappear without a trace, their bodies no doubt at the bottom of the numerous swamps back in the forest.

To this setting Carr and two companions came on a fall hunting trip some time before the murder, by chance spending the night in John Swimm's cabin. After a foray in the woods for deer before daybreak, they arrived back at the shack to find a young woman making buckwheat pancakes on the griddle for them. It was Olive Swimm.

"She was in absolute contrast to everything else about

the place," wrote Carr. "Her face was not pretty, but she had the build of a Venus. She was dressed in a plain gingham housedress beneath which her bare legs showed white as driven snow. Her jet black hair hung loose and accentuated the whiteness of her beautifully moulded neck. Her arms were bare and dimpled. There was plenty of fire in her dark brown eyes, and her mouth was well-shaped and her somewhat thick lips full and luscious as slightly over-ripe berries."

Olive, they heard later, had been the storm centre of love quarrels in that part of the country since she was twelve. She cared nothing for clothes or adornment, "All she had was a gloriously youthful body," and, wrote Carr a little waspishly, "her whole attitude advertised the fact that she was over-sexed."

Looking at John Swimm, scrawny and stooped with uneven, tobacco-stained teeth and a low forehead, and reminding Carr of a weasel, he found it hard to believe that this splendid young girl was his daughter. In fact, rumours were rife that she was the illegitimate offspring, farmed out to the Swimms, of well-to-do city folk.

While they ate their way through a pile of pancakes, pouring on home-made maple syrup and wild honey, the three hunters could hardly keep their eyes off Olive who, with her father, was tucking into the ham and beans the men had brought with them. One of the men, Roy, found Olive returning his bold glances, and when the hunters dispersed to the woods again after breakfast, Roy cannily offered to hang back and enter the woods near the farm to drive the game. As he left, Carr saw Olive come out of the shack with a rifle saying she'd walk a way with Roy and get some partridges for their dinner.

It was a poor day's hunting. As Carr walked through the infinite stillness of the woods listening to the leaves crackle and crunch under his boots, he heard a single rifle shot. When he got back to the shack, he was surprised to see that Roy's car had gone, and John Swimm told him Roy was waiting for him about a kilometre up the road. When he got there he found the windshield had been shattered and Roy sitting there in a jumpy condition.

He explained that he'd offered to take the gorgeous Olive for a short drive in his car and had parked on a wagon trail when, without warning, a bullet passed between their heads, shattering the windshield. Roy threw himself down on the seat, and Olive jumped out and ran down the road shouting, "Benny. . . . Benny. . . . Don't shoot again." It was their introduction to Benny Swimm, a man, as events would prove, who burned with jealousy.

Sleeping in the loft with the rest of the family, Benny had long been aware of Olive's physical attractions. In such surroundings the thought is the deed; they had long since found each other in carnal embrace, and now lived, accepted by the family, as husband and wife. But as she grew older and realized the power she exerted over men, Olive was reluctant to limit her favours to Benny, a skinny, unimposing fellow. Her fickleness led to many bitter arguments and threats, but Olive didn't change.

John Swimm eventually moved to Benton, south of Woodstock and near the Maine border, in search of better farmland, and Benny and Olive, their tempestuous affair on one day and off the next, moved from place to place. Then, at the end of February 1922, Olive met a big, dark-haired ex-soldier, Harvey Trenholm, who had been decorated in the war and who came to work at her brother's place in Benton where she was staying. He was all Benny wasn't—hard-working, reliable, physically attractive—and the glamour of the war still clung to him. Olive, seventeen years old and never more stunning, fell into his hand like a ripe peach.

Benny, sullen and upset, arrived at her father's place at Benton on March 13 and tried to see Olive, but was turned away. A couple of days later Olive and Harvey were married in the Baptist church at Meductic by the Reverend H.D. Worden, and went to live and work on a farm owned by a man named Sharp on Benton Ridge. The understanding was that Trenholm would buy the farm within a few weeks.

To Benny, it was as if a man had stolen his wife, and he knew what he must do. He sold his coat and vest to raise money, then went to Edward Estabrooks, the merchant at Rockland, and traded his rifle for a revolver with a faulty spring. On March 27 he walked the eight kilometres from Rockland to Hartland and caught the CPR train south. He got off at Woodstock and, wearing only the light raincoat and a cap, set out on the nineteen-kilometre hike to Benton. Alfred Ball, driving along with his team, gave him a lift part of the way.

"A fellow took my wife, and I'm going to look into it," he told Ball. Further along, he called on Jessie Kirk to ask the way to the Sharp farm and couldn't help telling her too the reason for his mission.

"I want to have them both arrested. It ain't right what he did," he said.

"They're married. Don't meddle with them," Mrs. Kirk advised.

"All they can do is kill me anyway," said Benny, half to himself.

"What might your name be?" she asked curiously.

"Benny Swimm," he said, and walked on towards the Sharp place. Sharp had gone to town that day, leaving Trenholm busy whittling maple sap tips while Olive worked at household chores. Happy as birds in the home that was soon to be theirs, they had no inkling that Benny was waiting outside as the afternoon darkened. And when Harvey Trenholm suddenly found himself looking into the barrel of the revolver, he had no chance to run: Benny shot him full in the face, and he dropped dead on the spot.

Olive ran to the kitchen door at the sound, only to be met by Benny holding the gun on her. He grabbed the collar of her cotton dress and ripped it open, then plunged the revolver between her breasts and fired. She staggered back into the kitchen, trying to get away from him, but he caught up with her in the living room and shot her again in the back, killing her.

Somewhere he found a pencil and a pad. He scrawled: "Good-bye, Olive Swimm," then added, "And sleep." He had to step past Trenholm's body, the blood already staining the snow, as he made his way to a sheep pen behind the farm. Shaking, sobbing, he took out the gun again, held it to his own head and fired. The blast knocked him over, and he felt the steady drip of his blood on the snow. But he felt, and that meant he was alive. He pulled himself up on the picket and gingerly felt his head. The bullet had struck his skull, deflected, and run under his skin, ending as a lump above his eye. He shuddered and checked the gun. There was one bullet left. He put the gun to his head again, then with a cry of mixed shame and anger at his lack of courage he stumbled away through the deep snow across the field.

Olive's brother was the first to find the bodies later that afternoon, and Sheriff Albion Foster was sent for from Woodstock. It was the next morning before the sheriff arrived on a horse-drawn sleigh he shared with the coroner, official photographer and reporters. The investigators quickly found the bloodstain in the sheep pen and followed the trail of blood through the snow to a house eleven kilometres away where Benny, his head now bound up in a rag, had come the night before asking for something to eat. At another house a little further on, he'd gone in early that morning asking if he could rest awhile. The sheriff found him upstairs in bed. His first words were: "Sheriff, this is awful. I suppose I will hang for it."

"It's awful what a woman can bring a man down to," he told one of the reporters as they took him back to the county jail in Woodstock. At his trial in April, Benny cut what one newspaper called "rather a neat figure" in a respectable brown suit, but he didn't have a hope. The defence tried to show insanity ran in the family, producing evidence that his grandfather had been subject to fits, and that one of his brothers, notoriously unbalanced, had stoned his own horse to death. When Benny was four years old, his mother testified, the same brother had chewed his face.

Benny took his death sentence quietly enough, but when he got back to his cell he began raving and had to be sedated. His execution, set for July 15, was postponed pending a psychiatric examination, but the doctors concluded he was sane, and the execution was set again for September 15.

Then a grim comedy took place: Sheriff Foster could not find a hangman to do the job. Ellise, the usual man, could not make the September date and sent back the deposit cheque, recommending a man named Holmes. Holmes was willing, but then broke his leg and couldn't appear. Finally, Foster had to get the court to delay another month while he went to Montreal to find a hangman. There he met a man named Doyle who assured him he'd taken care of a few in his time—although it turned out later he hadn't hanged anyone since before the war—and Foster, to be on the safe side, paid for a second hangman to be on the scene.

Woodstock today is almost exactly as it was in 1922, a Christmas-card scene of elegant New England-style houses with the jail and courthouse just as they were then. And a couple of blocks from the jail lives Ken MacLaughlen, eighty-two or eighty-three, he's not sure, a lawyer who came to Woodstock as a reporter for the Saint John *Globe* in October 1922 to cover the execution of Benny Swimm. A tiny figure, the image of the late New Brunswick tycoon Lord Beaverbrook, MacLaughlen perched himself on the edge of a Victorian velvet chair, looked out of the window, and remembered that day for me.

"I was staying at the Carlisle Hotel, and I got up that morning before 4:00 A.M., but by the time I got there there was already quite a number of people waiting outside the jail," he said.

Inside, as the judicial inquiry into the execution was later to hear, Sheriff Foster hadn't slept at all. Shortly after 4:00 A.M. he found Doyle awake and shaving. "I thought I would clean up," said Doyle nervously. The sheriff had given strict instructions that there was to be no drinking before the execution and, he said later, he saw no sign of drink on Doyle. When he went to get Doyle at 4:50 A.M., he told the hangman, "Now, Doyle, make no mistake."

Ken MacLaughlen, meanwhile, had been ushered into the death cell where two ministers were conducting "a lugubrious religious service. Ever since that day I have hated the two hymns we sang. I remember them now— 'What a friend we have in Jesus,' and 'Sin has left a crimson stain,' " he said with a tiny shudder. MacLaughlen had met the hangman, a loud-voiced, hearty fellow, the day before, but when he saw him now he was sure "he was either doped or drunk."

"Beat it!" the hangman told the ministers and officials in the cell.

"Are you the one?" Benny asked him.

"I'm the guy," said Doyle heartily. MacLaughlen remembered that Benny complained he was cold and had a sore throat, and one of the three attending doctors went to get him a sweater.

"He seemed at that moment a very inoffensive, pathetic little character," MacLaughlen recalled. At first Benny objected to having his arms pinned, but when Doyle said it was necessary he submitted, then walked awkwardly up the steps to the gallows which had been built behind a concealing fence in the prison yard about a metre from where the crowd stood.

"He was saying the Lord's prayer, I remember it, and Doyle told him, 'That's right, Benny, talk to God, he's the only friend you have got now,' " said MacLaughlen. "Benny had just got to, 'For Thine is the kingdom,' when Doyle sprang the trap. And as he dropped he swung against the side of the gallows with a thump."

Doyle came down the steps a few minutes later, saying in a loud voice, "Clean and pretty! Clean and pretty! That's how I like to see a job done." The crowd, hearing his words, stirred angrily. Four minutes after the trap was sprung, attending physician Dr. Thomas Griffin was under the gallows noting that Benny's pulse was still beating when he was cut down. He was lowered to the ground and the rambunctious Doyle declared, "He's dead as a doornail."

But when they carried him inside and laid him on a bench in the jail corridor, Griffin noticed his pulse was stronger. He was breathing lightly, and feeling his neck the doctor found it had been dislocated but not broken. Helplessly responding to a physician's instinct, he manipulated the neck to ease the pressure.

Outside the jail the crowd, perhaps hearing the news, was growing increasingly restive and angry with Doyle, and Foster told the hangman to get upstairs to a safe area of the jail. Benny began gasping as though he might come around at any moment. "It's just a death rattle," said one man. "No," said Griffin. "He's not dead. I could bring him back to consciousness."

"Well, the sentence has been carried out. He's been hanged by the neck," one said.

"No!" came Sheriff Foster's voice loud as thunder, and when everyone looked at him they saw tears streaming down his face. "The sentence of the court was that he will be hanged by the neck until dead, and he will be hanged by the neck until dead."

Sensing that the officials were hesitant about going on with their grisly task while he was there, reporter MacLaughlen went out to talk to the coroner's jury which was waiting to declare Benny officially dead. Meanwhile the two ministers who had come to pray now found themselves with a grimmer task. Together with the backup hangman, the men of the cloth carried the unconscious figure up the steps of the gallows and held him up while a noose was attached again around his neck.

"I heard the thud, and I knew it had happened," said MacLaughlen. An hour had passed since the first hanging. Dr. Griffin found Benny's neck broken, and when he was cut down fifteen minutes later he was well and truly dead.

The callous reaction of a few at the time—"Well, Benny

killed two people—it's only right he should have hung twice."

Within minutes after the second hanging, workmen were tearing down the scaffold, as if to erase the affair from the town's memory.

"It was a terrible thing," said Ken MacLaughlen later as we walked by the jail on a frigid January day. "I think everyone who had anything to do with it was pretty well shaken," and it may have been the harsh wind sweeping around the corner, but his misty blue eyes were watering.

Albert Guay:
The Great Pretender

A look of disgust crossed Albert Guay's slim, fastidious features. The attractive young woman sitting beside him on the plane was distinctly pale and was reaching for the motion sickness bag in front of her.

"Excuse me, Angel," he whispered to his young mistress as she buried her face in the bag. He slid out of his seat and found a window seat further down the aisle. He couldn't bear ugliness.

He stared out of the window at the blue St. Lawrence River thousands of metres below, and for the hundredth time went over in his mind the problem that tortured him: how to get rid of the one obstacle to his happiness—his wife Rita. Marie-Ange Robitaille, the young girl sitting a few seats back, was slipping away from him. For a time he'd been able to dazzle her by lavishing clothes on her during a shopping spree in Montreal, but Marie-Ange and her respectable working-class parents in Quebec City were adamant—if he couldn't marry her, he must give her up.

In desperation Albert had already made several attempts to get rid of the plump and comely, Spanish-featured Rita, who he'd married seven years before when they both worked at the St. Malo armoury in Quebec City during World War II. A young man to whom he had offered $500 to give her a glass of poisoned cherry wine had laughed in his face. And when a bomb had gone off in the Guay family car while Rita was driving, she had escaped unhurt, although a mechanic who had slipped into the driver's seat to make an adjustment had been maimed for life. No suspicion had fallen on Albert—he'd even done quite well claiming the car insurance. But the problem remained.

The idea of having Rita stabbed or shot made Albert feel sick. So messy! As the plane headed for Sept-Isles and what might be his last weekend of stolen bliss, Albert gazed down, trying to look for an answer in the broad river below.

As he escorted Rita down the steps from the plane a short time later, Albert's soft eyes were sparkling with confidence. He had worked it out. It was August 1949, and J. Albert Guay, aged thirty-one, a Quebec City jeweller, was about to commit Canada's worst single act of homicide, killing Rita—and twenty-two others. All without getting a spot of blood on his neatly manicured hands.

A few weeks later, on September 9, fisherman Patrick Simard listened idly to the drone of a plane in the sky as he worked near Sault-aux-Cochons, sixty-five kilometres from Quebec City. It was the Canadian Pacific Airlines DC3 on its way from Quebec City to Baie-Comeau on the St. Lawrence north shore, and Simard could almost set his watch by it every day. Suddenly there was an explosion. Simard looked up, and saw the plane falling out of the clear blue sky. It disappeared behind a hill, and he heard nothing more. "I thought perhaps I imagined the whole thing," he said later.

In Quebec City later that day reporter Roger Lemelin, soon to become a noted novelist and creator of TV's famous Plouffe Family series, was driving his blue Pontiac along the Grande Allée when he heard the names of the victims of the air crash announced on the radio.

"Why, that's Albert's wife," was his first reaction. The second thought that came into his mind—"Albert had something to do with that explosion."

What kind of man would immediately be suspected by his friends of having destroyed the lives of twenty-three people in one of the most cowardly crimes of the age? The answer, as it was in the case of Adolf Eichmann, was that Albert Guay was a monster of mediocrity.

"He acted out his life," Lemelin, now publisher of Montreal's *La Presse,* told me in his antique-furnished office. Guay lived in a world of his own imagining, creating roles, conveniently ignoring unpleasant facts, and now, eliminating twenty-three innocent people.

Guay, whose crime was to shock the postwar world, was a product of a particular time and place: Quebec City's lower town in the 1920s and 1930s. Forever in the shadow of the fortress hilltop city, it was a tough working-class ghetto from which few escaped. "We were prisoners of a closed community and our horizon was the cliffs above," said Lemelin. Some, like Lemelin and opera star Raoul Jobin, rose from the confines of the cliff-bottom slum on the wings of their talents; others, like Albert Guay and 1960s child murderer Leopold Guay, catapulted into the national limelight on the strength of their ghastly dreams of grandeur.

Albert Guay, said Lemelin, who now, significantly, lives in a cliff-top mansion, emerged with his two accomplices, a middle-aged woman named Marguerite Pitre and her crippled watchmaker brother Généreux Ruest, from "the mud of society." But as he grew up, the youngest of five children and the apple of his widowed mother's eye, life had seemed simple and agreeable. Whatever young Albert wanted, he got. Whether it was money for candies or a new bicycle, Mme. Guay always found the money to indulge her son. In his teens he hung around pool halls, earning money on the side selling watches on commission, and when World War

II came along he took a $40-a-week job operating a grinding machine at the armouries. A dashing figure, always well dressed, full of talk about his great schemes for getting rich, and driving a flashy Mercury, Albert was a favourite with the girls who worked at the armoury.

Lemelin remembers that his first meeting with Albert and Rita Guay was on their wedding day, when they came laughing and joking down rue Colomb, Albert resplendent in evening dress and top hat. In the working-class St. Saveur district, he looked like something out of a movie, and Lemelin thought, "There's a bluffer."

Guay, in fact, lived his life as if he were on-screen, dramatically embracing Rita on the sidewalk and kissing her with extravagant passion. And, said Lemelin, he even drove his car like a cowboy riding a horse, leaping out almost before it had come to a standstill. Albert's credo was: "I believe, therefore I am." If his car needed fixing, he would put on overalls, talk knowingly about engineering principles, undo every bolt in sight—then call a mechanic to repair the damage.

When the armoury closed at the end of the war, he opened a jewellery store, narrowing his eyes and talking with expertise whenever a watch was brought to him for repair. But as soon as the customer was out of the door he would turn it over to Généreux Ruest, a cripple who police were to describe as "a genius with his hands."

Posing as a well-to-do businessman also meant that he was an easy mark for anyone needing a loan, and neighbours even remembered him being ready and willing to drive a sick neighbour to hospital in the middle of the night. Albert, who neither drank nor swore, also made a big show of marching to Mass on Sunday with a prayer book under his arm.

But although he always talked in rosy terms about his business and set up small branch stores in Baie-Comeau and Sept-Isles, Guay was not prosperous. He was easily cheated by the salesmen who travelled to small communities selling his watches, and his dreams always outstripped his capabilities. Then he found a way to earn a little extra income.

On coming home one evening, he rushed out of his tenement apartment shouting, "I've been robbed, I've been robbed." Thousands of dollars' worth of watches had been taken, he said, and the insurance company took his word. After that there were more robberies—and a couple of fires—in his store, all of them conveniently insured. "I was born under an unlucky star," Albert would lament to his poker buddies, throwing his eyes up to the ceiling. "Fortunately, I was insured."

Albert's fantasies extended to his love life too. He soon became impatient with his role of husband and longed to be the carefree young blade he'd once been. For Albert, to wish was to be, so he was soon courting a young waitress, only seventeen, named Marie-Ange (Angel Mary) Robitaille, to whose parents he introduced himself as Roger Angers. ("Albert is not a very elegant name," Lemelin reported him as saying. "Now, Roger, that's a much better name.") Once again he was the young suitor, all hearts and flowers. But his dreams fell apart when Rita, suspicious of her husband, went to see the Robitaille couple.

"But he can't be married. He's talking of getting married to Marie-Ange. He even bought her an engagement ring," protested Marie-Ange's father. Rita showed them her wedding picture—and that settled it.

Albert, furious with his wife's interference, was unwilling to give up his fantasy. He settled Marie-Ange at first with Marguerite Pitre, the heavy-featured sister of Généreux Ruest to whom he had given a loan so that she could buy a roominghouse. Marie-Ange felt uncomfortable under the eye of the domineering older woman, and Albert later set up his child-mistress in a room of her own in lower town, forcing her to take the name Nicole Côté, not allowing her a key and keeping her a virtual prisoner.

For a time after that they lived in a room in Sept-Isles as M. and Mme. Guay, but Marie-Ange, realizing her affair with the possessive, big-talking jeweller was drifting, tried to free herself. She slipped from her room in lower town and boarded the sleeper train to Montreal. Guay marched into the ladies' room as she waited for her berth to be made up, picked up her bags, and she followed obediently back to the room that was almost her prison. He took away her shoes, hit her in the face and made red marks on her cheeks with his lips so that she would not want to be seen in the street.

Finally, Marie-Ange managed to free herself from Albert and returned to work as a waitress.

On her way to work the evening of St. Jean Baptiste Day, June 24, Marie-Ange heard footsteps running up behind her. It was Albert brandishing a revolver. He was depressed.

"Killing yourself is a lazy way out," she said.

"Maybe both of us will be lazy," he returned menacingly. Later, in the restaurant, Albert sprang out at her from the men's washroom in the basement, and after police were called he was taken away and charged with possessing a gun without a licence.

But Albert, tortured by desire for Marie-Ange, would not give up. Eventually, against all logic, she agreed to go to Montreal with him—providing he bought her a new wardrobe. It was another instance of the remarkable sway the slim jeweller held over others, persuading them by his fawning sincerity and braggadocio to act often against their own best interests to the point, it turned out, of aiding in murder and attempting suicide.

On his return to Quebec City, Albert, mindful of his new scheme to rid himself of Rita, went to see Généreux at his home, and asked casually how one would use a clock to explode dynamite. Généreux claimed later that Albert had wanted to blow up tree stumps on a property he'd bought at Sept-Isles. The watchmaker, a small, grizzled man with heavy eyebrows, drilled a hole in the face of an alarm clock and, using a battery and detonator caps supplied by Albert, made a detonating device for his old friend.

The morning of September 9 was a busy one for Albert. By 7:30 A.M. he was calling on Ruest to pick up a large box which he took to the Palais railway station, putting it into a locker. At 8:30 A.M. Marguerite Pitre arrived; Albert handed her the box and she caught a taxi to the airport.

"Drive carefully," she told the taxi driver. "There's a statue in the box. It's very fragile." The box, the driver was to remember, was about the size of a child's coffin.

Meanwhile Albert had taken Rita to the CP airline office at the Chateau Frontenac Hotel and was trying to persuade her to take the morning flight to Baie-Comeau to pick up some jewellery for him. The airline clerk was to remember that Rita Guay was reluctant to go, but Albert finally persuaded her and bought a ticket. He paid fifty cents extra for $10,000 flight insurance.

At the airport the parcel, addressed to a fictional "Alfred Plouffe" at Baie-Comeau, was accepted and stowed in the forward luggage compartment of the DC3. Captain Pierre Laurin started the engines, and at 10:30 A.M. the plane droned down the runway with nineteen passengers and three crew members on board. Fifteen minutes out, the explosion ripped through the luggage compartment without any warning, stunning or killing everyone aboard even before the shattered remains of the plane fell to a remote hillside. But Albert's great scheme, planned as he had gazed down at the river, had been to have the plane explode over water where there would be little evidence to indicate the cause of the explosion. Forestry workers who arrived at the plane site soon after detected the smell of dynamite. Among those killed were three top executives of the U.S.-owned Kennecott Copper Co., and police at first suspected they were the targets of an assassin.

In the city, as word came back that there were no survivors, Albert found a wonderful new role for himself: the bereaved husband. His sobbing broke the heart of everyone who heard him. He ordered the grandest funeral for Rita, and the coffin was crowned with an extravagant cross of lilies inscribed, "From Your Dear Husband." Greeting the stream of guests at the funeral parlour, he told Lemelin, "You know how much I loved her. But the important thing is she did not suffer. You don't think she suffered, do you?"

And when he heard the sobbing of another husband upstairs whose wife, the mother of three children, had died in the crash, Albert went to console the man. "Be brave, M. Chapados. Do as I do: put your trust in God. I have lost my young wife." At the graveside he told his little daughter, "Look, dear, Mama is leaving us forever," and was so overcome he had to be helped to a taxi.

But with Rita insured for $5,000 in addition to the $10,000 flight insurance, Albert was also thinking about new possibilities. He had Mme. Pitre invite Marie-Ange to her home, and the girl, always suspicious of the older woman, came reluctantly.

"Wait in here, dear," she said, showing Marie-Ange into the bedroom. From behind the door where he had been hiding, Albert emerged, glowing like a young bridegroom.

A few days later, the *Toronto Star* announced that the police were looking for a mysterious woman who had delivered a parcel to the plane shortly before takeoff. A copy of the story in his hand, Guay called on Mme. Pitre. "You had better do away with yourself," he told her, giving her some yellow sleeping pills and ordering her to turn on the gas taps. "And leave a note saying you were the one who blew up the plane." Oddly, Mme. Pitre took the pills—but she ended up in hospital charged with attempted suicide and with police at her bedside anxious to question her.

Within a few hours, Guay was arrested, and Généreux was admitting that—unwittingly—he had made the detonator for the bomb. At the trial, Albert was listless except when a pathologist described how every bone in Rita's body had been broken and her lungs had been burst in the explosion. Then he made a show of sobbing.

But when Marie-Ange, wearing a dark coat and a large, grey coachman's hat, stepped into the box, her dark lipstick accentuating the paleness of her face, Guay leaned forward, devouring every word. She told the story of their affair, breaking down at one point and saying, "I hate to do this. I don't want to hurt anyone. . . ." Her final answer to the lawyer's question was spoken softly. "No," she said. "I don't love him any more." The shadows that had enveloped the young girl—Albert's possessiveness, the frightening Mme. Pitre—were lifting at last. "I am going around with a nice boy now. I don't want to marry him until I have saved enough for a dowry, then I hope I will find some happiness," she told *Star* reporter Scotty Humeniuk.

In the courtroom Chief Justice Albert Sevigny wept as he called on the jury to fulfill the law of God, and in case jury members missed the point, he showed them a photograph of Rita Guay's broken body lying amongst the plane wreckage. The jury convened only seventeen minutes before delivering a verdict of guilt, and Judge Sevigny, describing the plot as "a diabolical, infamous crime," lost no time imposing the death sentence.

But the police had not finished. Three months later, armed with statements Guay had made in his death cell, they charged Ruest, the crippled watchmaker, with murder for his part in the crime. At the trial Ruest's sister, the dark and glowering Mme. Pitre, was dragged screaming from the courtroom after being charged with intimidating witnesses and uttering death threats in the witness waiting room.

With the testimony of a munitions worker that Ruest had phoned him for advice on how to detonate twenty sticks of dynamite, it became clear that Ruest knew more about the scheme than he had let on, and he too was sentenced to death, in December 1950.

The following month Guay the Pretender was led to the gallows. This time he proved inadequate for the role—he had to be supported on both sides by guards and died quaking.

Still the police had not finished. Mme. Pitre was charged with murder, and following the testimony of a hardware store clerk in lower town who had sold her twenty sticks of dynamite, she was also sentenced to death. On July 25, 1952, Généreux Ruest was trundled up to the gallows in Montreal's Bordeaux Jail in a wheelchair and lifted to a backless chair. Because one arm was paralyzed, they strapped one arm in front and one behind. The hangman, not accustomed to executing his victims in a sitting position, misjudged the length of the rope. It took the little watchmaker twenty-one minutes to choke to death.

Mme. Pitre, also known as Mme. Le Corbeau (Mrs. Crow) for the black clothes she always wore, went to the gallows January 9, 1953, after appealing her sentence to the Supreme Court of Canada.

And Marie-Ange? Middle-aged now, she has found her happiness living in a small community near Quebec City, her notoriety long forgotten. She is married to an ordinary man—not the actor Albert Guay who once impressed the locals at the ice cream parlour in lower town, storming up and down declaring: "You will hear more about me someday. I will make something of myself."

Shootout at Megantic

The dusty main street slumbering in the afternoon heat snapped to life; Nelson Leet, dozing in the rocking chair on the verandah of his hotel, shot forward and stared unbelievingly. On the upstairs balcony of Pope's Hotel, two chambermaids craned their necks to get a better view, and people going about their business froze in their tracks. In the American House Saloon, a man sidled up to Lucius "Jack" Warren.

"He's here," he said out of the side of his mouth. Warren turned pale, put his beer down unfinished and felt instinctively for the heavy revolver at his side. On the street, Donald Morrison, the tall cowboy with the Wyatt Earp moustache who had brought the town to this sudden state of nervous alert, nonchalently leaped a ditch and walked easily along the wooden sidewalk, slapping his leg with a small cane. Looking up, he noticed Warren coming out of the saloon towards him.

"I want to speak to you," said the lawman.

"Keep away!" said the cowboy, tight-lipped, but Warren

kept coming. "Keep away!" he called again and walked on purposefully until Warren barred his way.

"Keep away!" he said a third time. Then he saw Warren's hand drop and the blank eye of the revolver barrel come up towards him. People were dodging and dropping out of sight. In a blur the cowboy dropped his stick, snatched his Colt revolver, and in one smooth action sent a charge of lead smashing into Warren's throat, shattering his spine.

For a moment, as people crowded around the inert form of the lawman, the cowboy stood looking down. Then, dropping his gun back in its holster, Donald Morrison walked off down the street. No one raised a hand to stop him.

That's just the way it happened on June 22, 1888. Not in Dodge City or Laredo, but in the small town of Megantic in Quebec's Eastern Townships near the Maine border. Donald Morrison had ridden the ranges from Texas to Montana, but as he headed home to the soft, pine-covered hills east of Sherbrooke, he was destined to become a legend.

For one glorious year he became to the Scottish immigrants who came from the Isle of Lewis in the Hebrides to farm this stony, unyielding land a symbol of their pent-up anger against generations of oppressive landlords and money-lenders. They supported Morrison and hid him from scores of police and troops like their very own Bonnie Prince Charlie or Rob Roy. But in the end, of course, just as so many times before, they were tricked and defeated.

Donald Morrison, a Scottish hero in a countryside now alive with French–Canadian nationalism, is in danger of being forgotten; a historic plaque marking the site of the famous gunfight in what is now Lac Megantic was once erected and ceremoniously unveiled, but has since mysteriously disappeared. And as I drove over the rolling hills so familiar to Morrison during his fugitive year, I found a countryside inhabited by Scottish ghosts.

The villages have names like Scotstown, Lingwick and Stornaway, and the graveyards are full of Mackenzies and Mathesons and McDonalds. "But there's few of us Scots left here now," said sixty-four-year-old Duncan McLeod as he led me through the now-empty village store his grandfather built 103 years ago and upstairs to where he kept his mementos of the Morrison era. The few Scots left are mostly in their seventies or eighties, said McLeod, a leading light in the local historical society, and will soon be gone. And then who will remember Donald Morrison, a gunslinger and a killer, but a man who did what had to be done?

Morrison was the youngest child of Murdo and Sophia Morrison, who had come here from the Isle of Lewis in 1838, eventually settling on a fine 100-acre farm on a hilltop overlooking Lake Megantic. He was a child of middle-aged parents, but he wasn't spoiled: Malcolm Matheson, the storekeeper in Megantic, found him a hard and honest worker when, as a teenager, Donald helped him clear trees in the frontier town.

When he was eighteen, Donald, like many other youngsters of the era, felt the pull of the opening West and, with a friend, Norman MacAulay, rode out to be a cowboy. When he returned seven years later in 1883, the man who swung down from the train in Megantic and into his mother's arms had been transformed from an angular, awkward settler's son into a lean cowboy, tanned and moustached, with two Colt revolvers dangling from his hips.

Family troubles had brought Donald home: Murdo, now in his 70s, had become cantankerous with the years, had had disagreements with his other sons and was deep in debt. Donald, putting up with the old man's bad temper, worked clearing more farmland over the next few years and payed some of his father's debts from his savings.

But in 1886 Donald, having a beer one day in a Megantic bar, heard that his father without telling him had taken out a $1,100 mortgage with a hard-nosed former Union soldier and money-lender, Major Malcolm McAulay. Father and son had harsh words and Donald consulted a Sherbrooke lawyer named McLean.

"No problem at all, my boy," said the lawyer reassuringly. "All we do is sue your father—just a formality, mind—for that $900 you say you've put into the farm in money and labour. Then, when the farm is put up for sale to cover the debts, we'll buy it for a nominal amount, and you'll just take over the mortgage. Simple!"

But when Donald got home and talked it over with his father, he found matters were worse than he'd thought. Murdo, unable to read and write in English, had been cheated by McAulay, who had advanced him only $700 of the $1,100 face value of the mortgage.

"There it is, read it for yourself," said McAulay confidently when Donald stormed into his office next day for an explanation. Sure enough, the agreement allowed McAulay to hold back $400 towards future payments. "But," spluttered Donald, "that means my father is paying nine percent interest on money he didn't get!"

"That's right," said McAulay. "Good day."

Black with anger, but helpless, Donald waited for the day when his father's farm would be put up for auction. Lawyer McLean, acting for Donald, opened the bidding at $200. But McAulay, from the back of the room, upped it to $1,000. Donald felt his world crumbling; he nodded at McLean, who increased the bid to $1,100.

"Sold!" said the sheriff, who was conducting the sale. "Now will that be cash or cheque?" McLean stepped forward and whispered in the sheriff's ear that they'd need a few days to pay.

"Sorry," said the sheriff, shaking his head. "If you don't have the money, the farm goes to the next highest bidder. Major McAulay, would you step forward here a moment, please."

McAulay soon had the legal wheels turning to evict Murdo and Sophia, and Donald finally found them a dilapidated log cabin on a few scrubby acres on the outskirts of Marsden (now called Milan). By the following summer McAulay had sold the old Morrison homestead to Auguste Duquette who, unaware of the legal battle, moved his family into the Morrisons' old place.

Twice Donald told Duquette to get off the farm, but the sturdy Auguste took no notice. Then, in May 1888, Duquette's stable burned down in the night. The following week Mme. Duquette was about to wind the clock in the kitchen when a bullet shattered the window and smashed into the clock face. Duquette went to the police in Megantic and moved his family across the road for safety. It wasn't a moment too soon: a few days later during Auguste's absence the old Morrison home burned down.

Donald and his friends denied responsibility, and he claimed he could prove he was in another part of the country when at least two of the incidents had occurred. But it looked awfully suspicious, and a warrant was sworn out for Donald's arrest. For a while nothing happened. Local police had no stomach for arresting Donald when the whole countryside felt the Morrisons had been cheated out of their farm. Eventually a whisky smuggler from across the United States border, Jack Warren, fancying there was a reputation to be made capturing the elusive Morrison, got a reluctant justice of the peace to swear him in as a special constable. Warren immediately began playing his new role to the hilt, telling sceptical tipplers at the local hotels that he'd bring Morrison in dead or alive, and soon Megantic echoed to the sound of gunfire as Warren set up a target behind Pope's Hotel and began honing his sharp-shooting skills.

Morrison, kept up-to-date by his friend Malcolm Matheson, stayed out of the way of the trigger-happy smuggler, spending his time in the bush and making regular rendezvous with Augusta McIver, an attractive young farm girl he hoped to marry. Then, on June 22, believing Warren was out of town, Morrison came striding easily down Megantic's main street—and into big trouble.

As Morrison was walking away after the shootout with Warren, Matheson, having witnessed the affair, was in the back room of his store writing down the names of half a dozen reliable people who, he decided, would form the nucleus of the Morrison Defense Organization. In the next eleven months, as the hunt for Donald went on, the organization would swell to include almost every Scot and many of the French–Canadians in Compton County.

Detectives and, later, troops were brought in from Quebec City and Montreal, and the rare charge of "Outlawry"—used also against the rebel Louis Riel in western Canada—was invoked. But wherever the officers turned they were greeted with blank faces and shaking heads when they enquired about Morrison.

Peter Spanjaardt, a Dutch-born reporter for the Montreal *Star* who arrived in Megantic the day after the shooting, soon realized that the key to contacting Morrison was through Malcolm Matheson, the taciturn, heavily bearded storekeeper. When Spanjaardt informed Matheson he wanted to interview Morrison, the Scot shrugged. "I canna help you," he said shortly. It was only after Spanjaardt wrote a sly, humorous article about the bumbling efforts of the police to find their quarry that, one morning as he was eating breakfast at his hotel, Matheson walked up to the table and told him to get himself on board the 7:30 A.M. train to Sherbrooke and get off the first time the train stopped.

Spanjaardt left his breakfast and caught the train with seconds to spare. Just outside town the train began to slow; then, as the reporter leaped off, it picked up speed again. "This Morrison has friends everywhere," Spanjaardt thought to himself. But as the reporter waited for several hours on the road nearby, he began to wonder if he'd been made a fool. Just then he heard jingling harness, and around the corner came Matheson in a buggy. "Climb up," he said gruffly, and they went on their way in silence.

The two travelled most of the day with Matheson gradually becoming more forthright as he got to know the reporter. Towards the end of their journey, Spanjaardt was alarmed to see armed men coming out of the woods to hold heated discussions with Matheson in Gaelic before they were allowed to go on.

At last they arrived at a small house hidden in the trees,

and Spanjaardt was shown into the parlour. The door opened, and he found himself facing Donald Morrison. "I unconsciously looked at his trousers to see if his murderous weapons were in his pockets," Spanjaardt wrote afterwards, somewhat melodramatically. "His hands were free and he stretched out his hand with the cordial words, "I am Morrison, how are you?"

He nervously offered the outlaw a cigar; then, without the need for prompting, Morrison began striding up and down telling him of the sequence of events that led to the showdown at Megantic. As the outlaw talked, Spanjaardt was taking in his appearance: "A tall, gaunt, big-framed Scotchman with a ruddy complexion and steel-blue eyes, high cheekbones, tawny moustache and a rather serious mien which, however, was lightened at times by a specially charming smile."

At the end Spanjaardt asked the question Morrison knew was inevitable: "Someone shot through Duquette's window and fired his stable and house. Was that you?"

Morrison looked him directly in the eyes. "No. It was not. I did not do the shooting, and I can prove that during the burning of the stable I was in Spring Hill and during the burning of the house, in Hampton."

Summer turned to fall and fall to winter and Quebec Premier Honoré Mercier fumed at the outlaw who was making a laughing stock of his government as more and more police and soldiers were drafted into the hunt. Morrison appeared to be everywhere—and nowhere.

Coming around a corner one day in midwinter, a group of policemen trudging along trying to forget their cold and misery saw a solitary snow-shoer coming towards them. "Good day," he shouted cheerily, and the greeting was returned.

"Hey," said one puzzled officer as the stranger passed, "Are you Donald Morrison?" The man roared with laughter. "If I was, would I be standing here talking to you?" he said, and Morrison went on his way chuckling.

Another day police arrived just as Morrison was having

tea with a Mrs. Campbell at Magill Lake. "Quick, get under the couch, Donald," she said as she spotted the blue uniforms outside. She deftly wiped off the extra cup, put it back on the shelf, then opened the door to the police. But as the officers looked over the little house she noticed that Donald's boots were sticking out. She edged over to the couch, sat down casually, covering the boots with her skirts, and said something in Gaelic to one of the officers. "Sorry, ma'am, I don't understand Gaelic," he said, and they left a few moments later. The two could hardly stop laughing as she helped him out from under the couch. In their own language she'd said, "Pull in your feet."

In Quebec City the premier had had enough of this sort of nonsense. Judge Aimée Dugas, a tough and fearless law enforcer, was put in charge of a new force of some 300 policemen, soldiers and even prison guards that arrived April 7, 1889, in Morrison country. Dugas immediately locked up three men suspected of aiding Morrison and had forty-five more warrants drawn up ready for use against members of the Morrison Defence Organization.

Augusta McIver, during clandestine meetings, had been urging Donald to leave that part of the country, perhaps to go out West again, but he insisted he would stay until he got justice. With Matheson's encouragement, he agreed to meet Dugas during a temporary truce to see if there was any hope of compromise. The two men met in a small schoolhouse near Gould, shaking hands, then fitting awkwardly into the school desks to talk.

"Give up now. You can't win," Dugas told him.

Morrison shook his head. "I'll not give up unless all the charges against my friends and myself are dropped," he said. Other than that, he would agree to leave the country—if McAulay paid him the $900 he felt he was owed on the farm deal.

Dugas got up. There was nothing more to say. They shook hands and the judge left without a word. The next morning Dugas sent his officers out with orders to round up the other forty-five Morrison supporters named on the warrants.

The stubborn settlers still left their kitchen doors open at night with food on the table for Donald, and in Quebec City the influential Caledonian Society, representing upper-crust Scots, was working behind the scenes to effect another truce during which, its leaders hoped, they could make a deal with Morrison. A deputation from the society arrived in Sherbrooke on Good Friday, April 19, with the premier's agreement for an Easter truce. Dugas was briefed and agreed to meet Morrison again on Easter Monday. That Sunday there was good news for the Scots as their preachers announced in the little country kirks that a new truce at last offered the promise of a settlement.

Oddly enough, with so much afoot, Judge Dugas and High Constable Adolphe Bissonette, now in charge of police operations, left the area for the weekend after giving Chief Detective Silas Carpenter of the Montreal police a briefing at their hotel Saturday morning. Carpenter, in turn, went to Murdo and Sophia's cabin to give instructions to men staked there waiting for Morrison. There could have been little word of "truce" in their instructions, for when Donald arrived at the cabin on Sunday to fetch his best clothes for his planned meeting with Dugas on Monday, Constable James McMahon and Pierre LeRoyer, a French trapper who had joined the hunt for the sake of the $3,000 bounty on Morrison's head, were crouched in the bush nearby.

McMahon, creeping forward to peer through the window, saw a man straddling a chair and eating, his back to the window. Sophia handed him a bottle of milk and some biscuits and held his hand, and the man turned. "That's our man," breathed McMahon, and they flattened themselves against the barn wall.

McMahon claimed afterwards that as Morrison came out of the door he shouted to him, "Hold up your hands!" and that the outlaw fired several shots "and ran like a deer."

Other accounts suggest he was fired on without warning. In any case, Morrison was brought down with a bullet in the hip and they were on him in a flash.

Marsden Station that night seemed more like a battle-front to reporter Spanjaardt than a quiet little Quebec town on a Sunday. Hundreds of soldiers and policemen were massed at the approach to the station, fingering their guns nervously in anticipation of a counterattack from the local Scots. He found Morrison lying on the floor of the waiting room in desperate pain, no one paying any attention to his wound as they waited for a special train which was to carry him to jail in Sherbrooke.

At Stornaway, Dr. J.H. Graham, heading the Caledonian Society deputation, was close to tears. "We have been deceived and Morrison has been betrayed during a pretended truce," he said. Clarke Wallace, who spent months going over diaries, police and newspaper reports for his authoritative book on Donald Morrison, told me: "There's no doubt at all in my mind. It was a set-up."

Six months later, Morrison, still limping from his wound, went on trial in Sherbrooke, and his friends noted that his face was lined and aged beyond his thirty-one years. After the jury had deliberated for twenty-four hours on the murder charge, the foreman, Camille Millette, announced that Morrison had been found guilty, but with a recommendation that the lightest sentence be handed down. A shock went through the courtroom as Judge Edward Brooks announced that Morrison would serve eighteen years hard labour in the St. Vincent de Paul penitentiary. "Good God!" said Camille in the stunned silence that followed the sentencing. "We never expected that."

Four years later, a broken, unrecognizable figure emerged from the penitentiary. Morrison, whose soul had seemed to shrivel in the harsh jail, was helped into a clergyman's carriage by supporters from the Caledonian Society and was taken directly to the Royal Victoria Hospital where he died hours later.

He came home like a hero, his burial paid for by the Caledonian Society, and a long procession of friends and dignitaries followed the coffin up the bush road from his parents' cabin in Marsden to Guisla Cemetery. "He died of consumption—and a broken heart," said Duncan McLeod, putting away his mementos as I prepared to leave. Outside, the previous night's snowstorm had piled the banks high, almost obliterating the houses in the little village.

"You'll not be able to drive up the Guisla road today, Duncan warned. "No one lives there now. The cabin is gone—it's only a depression in the ground."

I turned my car into the lane leading to the cemetery, past fields that have long since been reclaimed by pine and balsam trees. The air was knife-cold as I waded through the snow in the graveyard.

One stone said simply: "Morrison." Then my foot struck something beneath the snow. I dug down and discovered a smaller stone. "Donald Morrison," it said, and gave the date of his death as 1889—the year of the trial. Was it a mistake on the part of the stonemason? I think not—in one sense Donald Morrison died the day the penitentiary gates closed on him. Yet in another sense, he is still alive in the soft wind soughing through the pine trees on these gentle hills.

The Judge Who was Tried
for Murder

My fingers wrap comfortably around the stock of the
clumsy pistol. I raise the pistol slowly to arm's length,
pointing it through the window at a snowy courtyard scene
in old Perth, Ontario, that hasn't changed in 150 years. And
in that instant my hand trembles, the scene blurs, and I
become John Wilson, a young law student holding this very
pistol, scared and sick to his stomach as he prepares to take
another's life—or lose his own.

Today the portrait of Judge John Wilson hanging in
Toronto's Osgoode Hall, hallowed home of the Upper Canada Law Society, reveals a beefy, ruddy-faced Victorian, a
much-honoured and worthy example to aspiring young
lawyers. But few of those young lawyers would realize that
Wilson holds a unique distinction: he was tried for murder
in the very courtroom where he later presided as judge.

Wilson's poignant story is still very much alive in the
stone walls and colonial buildings of this handsome old
town southwest of Ottawa—if you know where to look. On

an old wall on Gore Street, you can still make out the fading sign, "Radenhurst, Barrister," where Wilson's nineteen-year-old victim, Robert Lyon, worked as a law student. Up the hill, "The Summit House," where the twenty-three-year-old lived under the roof of his employer, still peers down on the town with a dowager's disdain.

A few blocks away in a magnificent 1823 stone house named "Ingeva," a Perth grande dame, Winnifred Inderwick, prepared an aromatic beef broth for our lunch in the kitchen—it was a bedroom then—where the lifeblood, say some, drained from Robert Lyon's body.

It was a ridiculous murder—a game of make-believe with a horribly real ending. It was an affair of honour, of young dandies preening and prancing like puffed-up game cocks and pretending to grand emotions—until Robert Lyon fell back into the mud with a bullet in his chest while the rain ran down his still face. But in its way, the killing of Robert Lyon mirrored the pressures and antagonisms that four years later were to explode to shape the Papineau–Mackenzie Rebellion of 1837 against the priggery of Canada's ruling British "Family Compact." It was a murder that would follow John Wilson even as he pushed to the top as a legislator and as a judge.

Perth in 1833 was a mere twenty years old. But far from the kind of let's-pull-together pioneer community we popularly imagine such young towns in the wilderness to have been, it simmered with conflicts, snobbishness and class distinctions. The town had been established in the wake of the War of 1812, when the British realized that their line of communications along the St. Lawrence River could easily be broken by American forces crossing the river. Perth was established to settle the frontier with discharged soldiers and half-pay officers who would provide a loyal population to protect an alternate transportation route along the Ottawa and Rideau Rivers.

At the same time a wave of poor Scottish and Irish immigrants arrived and quickly found themselves at the bottom of the pecking order in a community dominated by the

Family Compact officer class. Typical of this was the case of William Bell, a Presbyterian clergyman who identified with the newly arrived Scots and had founded Perth's first school—only to have it taken from him and handed over to an upper-class Episcopalian.

In his journal, the most important document on Perth's early history, Bell deplores "the haughtiness, pride, vanity and dissipation of the half-pay officers and their ladies. They minded nothing but dress, visiting and amusements."

Robert Lyon, Scottish-born but related to the Radenhursts, the Ridouts and the Jarvises of the Family Compact, belonged to one side of the great class divide in Perth, while Wilson, the son of a Scottish weaver, belonged to the other.

Wilson's father, Ebeneezer, brought his family from Scotland in 1819 and hacked a farm out of the wilderness thirty-two kilometres from Perth. In spite of his humble background, he was known as a man of wide reading and strong opinions, traits he passed on to John, his oldest son by a second marriage.

Young Wilson, determined from the start to get ahead, began his own school in Perth, at the same time keeping the books for a local merchant—even when it meant staying up late at night and working by the light of the fire when he could not afford candles. In 1829 Wilson articled as a law student to James Boulton, agreeing to pay his way by tutoring Boulton's son before going to work in the law office each morning and, presumably at the end of his work day, tutoring the children of another prominent local family.

The dawn-to-dusk labours of the short, burly Scottish law student contrasted vividly with the easier life of other legal trainees he encountered, notably Robert Lyon and Henry Lelievre, who both worked for Radenhurst. Lelievre, the son of a former French naval officer, was something of a fop and was later described by a contemporary as "a well-dressed, idle nobody."

By contrast, Wilson was given to writing homilies in his journal about hard work and dedication and even approached the lighthearted business of love with a rather tedious earnestness. "As nature or, rather, inclination, has not fitted me for shining in the female circle, I must content myself with the hope of one day meeting a female who has sense enough to value worth altho' stript of the gaudy glitter of a well-bred coxcomb," he consoled himself.

But Wilson was nothing if not determined. He turned his amorous attentions first to Joanna Lees, the daughter of a local miller, presenting her, as was proper for a young man already prominent in the Presbyterian church, with a small religious book on her sixteenth birthday. Their friendship warmed, and it was assumed they would marry. But in 1832 there arrived in Perth a young woman of more spectacular charms, Elizabeth Hughes, touchingly arrayed in black in memory of her father, a Unitarian minister, who had died of cholera in Quebec.

Wilson soon switched his attentions to Miss Hughes, who had become a teacher at a ladies' academy—schooling seems to have been Perth's major activity at this period—run by her guardian, Gideon Ackland. Wilson was warned by Ackland that Miss Hughes had no corresponding feeling of warmth for the young law student, but he continued to press ahead.

On February 14, 1833, we find him penning a valentine to Elizabeth Hughes, declaring:

> This world, tho' large, is nothing without you.
> But talking's vain when little's in my power,
> Then I'll be silent till a happier hour,
> And should that happier hour never be mine,
> I'll mourn my lost, my dearest Valentine.

While the muse was upon him, he dashed off another missive the same day to Caroline Thom, a young relation of James Boulton, that began:

> Pretty darling little sprite!
> Oh! Thou ray of purest light.

Wilson was transferred to Bytown—soon to become Ottawa, Canada's capital—to run James Boulton's branch office there, and that left the field open for Henry Lelievre to press his attentions on Miss Hughes. He made such great strides that Ackland felt it necessary to warn her that the bounder's intentions were probably not honourable, and she agreed to break off the connection.

Lelievre and Lyon, suave young men-about-town, missed no chance to make fun of the serious, solemn Wilson with his humble background, and when Lyon met Wilson in Bytown he decided to have a bit of fun at Wilson's expense.

Why, he said, Elizabeth Hughes had not broken off with Lelievre at all.

"Oh?" said Wilson, his jealousy aroused.

"No," said Lyon. As a matter of fact he, Lyon, had recently taken Caroline Thom and Miss Hughes for a walk during which they had a slyly prearranged encounter with Lelievre. And, said Lyon, watching the colour rise to Wilson's face, before long Miss Hughes was sitting with Lelievre's arms around her "in a position which no woman of spirit would permit."

Wilson strode away, trying to hide his anger. When he got back to his lodgings, he could not resist writing to Miss Hughes's guardian, Gideon Ackland, to reveal what Lyon had told him. Concerned about proprieties, Ackland made inquiries, and soon the contents of Wilson's letter were common knowledge.

Now it was Lyon's turn to be angry: Ackland and Miss Thom wanted to know what he had been up to, and his explanation that it was all a joke on poor old Wilson didn't sound very convincing.

A few days later Lyon encountered Wilson on the street in Perth.

"Did you write that letter to Ackland?" he demanded.

"Yes, but . . ." Before the words were out of his mouth, Wilson found himself flat on his back reeling from Lyon's blow.

"You're a damned lying scoundrel!" Lyon told him.

Pulling himself to his feet, Wilson offered to go to Gideon Ackland so that they could sort out the whole thing.

"I'll go to no person with you," said Lyon, and turned on his heel.

Wilson heartily disapproved of duelling, but he realized that without a confrontation he would become the laughing stock of Perth. Common sense fought against pride, but finally he appointed a fellow student, Simon Robertson, as his second. Because Robertson was a friend of Lyon's, he hoped for a reconciliation.

Indeed, the details of an agreement—with Lyon offering an apology and Wilson clarifying the intent of his letter— were worked out. But Lyon, perhaps egged on by his second, Lelievre, backed out of the agreement at the last moment. Lelievre, knowing that Lyon was an expert shot and that Wilson abhorred guns, saw the duel as a splendid means of getting rid of Wilson—his rival for Miss Hughes's affections.

At 5:00 P.M. on June 13, word flashed around the town: Wilson and Lyon had been seen walking towards the river together. The site chosen for the duel was a ploughed field on the banks of the River Tay—conveniently across the town line where the local sheriff, a friend of both participants, would not have the embarrassing duty of arresting them.

The two men walked stiffly, ignoring the rain dripping down their faces. Wilson found it an effort to quell his mounting fear, conscious as he was of his lack of skill with firearms. Lyon was no less fearful—twice in the preceding days he'd woken in a sweat after dreaming that he was walking past the burial ground wearing a shroud.

Several people, braving the rain, were hurrying after them to witness the exciting event. James Boulton had been in his office when a man burst in to tell him the two young men were on their way to the river.

"I'll go home and get my coat and come with you," said Boulton.

"If you do, you might be too late to stop it," he was told, so Boulton went as he was. He was a ways off when he saw the duelists taking up their positions. Horrified, he saw an umbrella thrown to the ground—the signal to fire.

The guns exploded simultaneously. Boulton, peering through the rain, saw two puffs of smoke. The smoke cleared, and he breathed a sigh of relief. Both men were still standing. In these affairs, one exchange of fire was usually accounted enough, and apologies usually followed. With this in mind, Dr. William Hamilton, the surgeon in attendance, hurried forward and asked the seconds to stop the affair for a few minutes with a view to reconciliation.

"That's impossible," said Lelievre.

"Then let me speak to Lyon," said the doctor.

Lelievre said that wasn't possible either until the guns were loaded. "However," Hamilton was to testify, "I went to Lyon and said, 'For God's sake, Lyon, is there no way to put a stop to this unfortunate business?' "

"Doctor, it's impossible," said Lyon.

Hamilton rushed over to Wilson and Robertson and found them ready to exchange apologies and forget the matter. But as he started back towards the others, Hamilton saw that Lyon was taking up his position with the gun in his hand. There was nothing further he could do.

Wilson grasped the heavy pistol and took up his position. He noticed Lelievre talking quietly to Lyon and pointing. Suddenly it dawned on him that Lelievre was pointing out the plough furrow which led in a direct line between the two duelists. It was the perfect gunsight.

With an awful premonition, said Wilson, "I saw Lyon's pistol pointed in a direct line with my body and thought I should fall." His body shuddered, and suddenly he felt sick. The bystanders had become silent. The umbrella fell again. Wilson turned his head away and squeezed the trigger, expecting it to be his last act on earth.

Again the two guns exploded. As the smoke cleared, Wilson was amazed to find himself standing and unhurt. But Lyon was collapsing into the mud. The doctor rushed over: the bullet had pierced the right side of the chest.

There is conflicting evidence about what happened next. Dr. Hamilton said Lyon died within a few minutes; other witnesses say Lyon was carried to the house now called "Ingeva" where his employer, Thomas Radenhurst, lived, and died there as a servant was sent next door for rags to staunch the blood. The Reverend William Bell reported seeing the body in a farmhouse near the fatal spot where two magistrates and a jury conducted an inquest while Thomas Radenhurst sat beside the bed "drunk, crying and swearing by turns and abusing Mr. Boulton and all his connections."

Lelievre fled the area and eventually moved to Australia. But Wilson and Robertson were lodged in the debtor's cell in the Perth courthouse and went on trial for murder in Brockville August 8, 1833.

In the American West in the years that followed, the gun was to become law, and few were brought to justice for killing others in gunfights which were, essentially, duels. But in Upper Canada it was called murder, and the fact that Wilson and Robertson were charged may have been one reason that gunfighting never became a popular means of settling grudges in this country.

The evidence was clear, and Wilson made little attempt to excuse himself. He related how, with a terrible inevitability, events had sped to that moment when "I felt the dreadful reality of my situation, expecting to be killed." But death itself was less terrifying than the reproaches of his friends and a scornful world, he said.

The judge, Mr. Justice James McAuley, came down hard against duelling; but, he pointed out, Wilson had always expected to reach an amicable settlement. "He went out determined not to fire at the deceased and did so at last in a state of convulsive nervousness," he said.

The jury quickly found both men not guilty and, as the irascible Bell noted, "The jury . . . were Irish, who consider fighting commendable rather than a crime."

Wilson, his lesson learned, renewed his attentions to Joanna Lees, writing her long letters, pleading for a second chance in the months following his acquittal. But her parents were outraged at his behaviour and firmly opposed the connection.

Then an act of natural justice intervened. Following the duel, Elizabeth Hughes's reputation had been left in tatters, and when Gideon Ackland fell into financial difficulties her future became bleak. Perhaps seeing himself as Sir Galahad, Wilson proposed, and they were married in the spring of 1835.

The couple moved first to Niagara and then to London, Ontario, where Wilson built a fortresslike house, "Elmhurst."

He prudently toed the establishment line, becoming a captain in the militia in the 1837 rebellion and, in 1847, a member of parliament. The member he succeeded, William Draper, had prosecuted him for murder fourteen years before, and his parliamentary leader, Henry Sherwood, had been his defence counsel.

In 1849, when Tories gloated at the burning of the Parliament Buildings in Montreal, Wilson renounced Toryism, returned to his roots and became a Reformer. He had a distinguished political career, was noted for his blunt, plain-spoken and honest approach, and in 1863 he was appointed to the bench.

He learned, with mixed feelings, that his first assizes would be in the Brockville courthouse. Entering the building on September 29 of that year, the memories crowded in on him. On that day the Crown counsel, later Mr. Justice Britton, entered the judge's chambers. Years later, he still remembered the scene that greeted him. Judge Wilson was walking up and down, wringing his hands and crying like a baby.

"Mr. Britton," he said. "The last time I was in this courthouse, I was on trial for murder."

Two weeks later Wilson returned to Perth for the assizes there and, in the grand welcome from members of the bar and in Wilson's gracious response, there was not a hint of the circumstances of previous events in Perth. But the duel was never far from his mind, and he found his way to the old burial ground on Craig Street where Lyon's gravestone bore the inscription:

> Friendship Offering Dedicated to the Memory of ROBERT LYON (Student-at-Law). He fell in mortal combat, 13th of June, 1833, in the 20th year of his age. Requiescat in Pace.

We had talked through lunch and on into the afternoon about Wilson and the young man who had lain in the next room, and now Winnifred Inderwick led me from the splended Colonial dining room at Ingeva into her study. She took out a tiny black box that opened into a woman's small writing desk with pens and inkwell.

"It belonged to Joanna Lees," she said. "I believe Wilson gave it to her."

I leaned over, pulled open the drawer, and a smell of long ago escaped—musty, and yet mixed with romance.

"He could never forget," said Mrs. Inderwick. "All through his life he would write to Joanna's mother, going over the events that had happened."

On his last visit to Perth for the assizes of April 1866, John Wilson met Joanna again, though it is nowhere written what regrets they may have expressed to each other. He wrote again to Mrs. Lees a long rambling letter about the past, concluding, "Would that I could justify the errors of my life and have your forgiveness. I must let that pass which I cannot recall. Nor must other ears hear how deeply I feel the wrong."

Three years later Wilson died in his home at London. He was fifty-nine. Elizabeth Hughes Wilson, who became a member of the fundamentalist Plymouth Brethren, died in Toronto in 1904 at the age of ninety-three.

"She led him a miserable life, as I heard it," said Mrs. Inderwick, gently closing the little writing desk where his last letter to Mrs. Lees had been found. "Oh, these stupid affairs of honour!"

Who Poisoned Percy Bell?

Percy Bell's face was flushed and perspiring as he collapsed into the chair after the unaccustomed exertion of tap-dancing. "Phew! I haven't done that for years," he panted.

"Now, Percy," cried his wife Mary. "Last tune of the evening and it's your request. What do you want Rusty to play?" Roscoe "Rusty" Jenners, a dapper little barber, tuned the new fiddle that the Bells had given him for Christmas while he waited for Percy to make up his mind.

"I know," said Percy, " 'Abide With Me.' That was always my favourite." And so, as the final hours of New Year's Day 1954 ticked away, the four of them—the Bells, Rusty and his mother—all having enjoyed a hearty supper of turkey and cranberry sauce, raised their voices in harmony:

> Abide with me! fast falls the eventide;
> The darkness deepens; Lord, with me abide:

"Oh my!" sighed Mary as they drove home through Belleville, Ontario's silent streets afterwards to the big house on Albert Street where Rusty roomed with them. "I think that was the most wonderful Christmas and New Year's we've ever had." Percy, festive and glowing, nodded. The clouds indeed seemed to be rolling away; a month before he'd had bad back trouble, the fellows at the factory had noticed he was edgy and irritable, and to top it all, Mary had come home one day and told him that her fortune teller, Madame Cleo, had predicted he would die in six to eight weeks.

If the news had troubled Percy, Mary at least took the jocular view. "No sense buying Percy a new suit now," she joked with her sister, Mrs. Penrose Caird. "He wouldn't get the wear out of it."

As they entered the house, Mary offered: "I feel like a little nightcap, how about you boys?"

"Don't mind if I do," said Rusty, but Percy declined and Mary went to make two gin and ginger ales as the two men settled down to watch late-night wrestling on television.

"You know," said Percy, rubbing his back around the kidneys, "I think my back is playing up again."

"I'll get you your liver pills," said Rusty, and when he brought the bottle Percy took one out and swallowed it.

At midnight, with the last of the big bruisers bounced out of the ring, Percy declared, "Well, I'm for bed," and went downstairs to check the furnace before they all went upstairs to bed.

Rusty was fast asleep at 2:00 in the morning when he was awakened by Mary's frantic call, "Come quick and help me, Rusty. Percy's awful sick." In the Bells' neat back bedroom with the blue-flowered wallpaper, he found Percy retching and vomiting in agony.

"I had to phone all over town before I could get a doctor," said Mary in anguish. "Oh, Rusty, what can we do?" At that moment the bell rang downstairs and Mary hurried down to let in Dr. Reg Anderson, the physician she had reached. "Come in, doctor, I've been trying to get someone since midnight," she said.

Anderson found his patient in a dire condition: his chest was covered with scratch marks where he'd clawed himself in his agony. A few minutes after the doctor arrived, Percy went into convulsions and died. Going downstairs afterwards, the doctor noticed that the breakfast table had been set for three—a small item that was to weigh heavily in the sensational trial of Mary Elizabeth Bell for the murder of her husband. But for now, there was no suspicion of foul play, and the doctor, although a little puzzled at the symptoms, put down "cerebral haemorrhage" as the cause of death on the death certificate.

Mary went to pick out a burial plot with a fine view of the boats passing on the river the next day at Riverside Cemetery in Napanee. "I want him buried like a prince," she insisted. With the marble headstone, Percy's stylish funeral cost close to $1,000.

But people in this handsome old Loyalist town on the north shore of Lake Ontario were remembering odd little things, and rumours began circulating. The Bells' daughter, Mrs. Earl Tiverton, for example, recalled her mother saying a few weeks before Percy died that he was in bad health, "and might die at any time like the snap of a finger. But don't let on to Percy. It's better he shouldn't know," she had warned. On the day of the funeral, Mary's sister and her husband, the Cairds, who had their own suspicions about Mary's relationship with Rusty, informed the Ontario Provincial Police that there was something suspicious about Percy's death.

A crack investigator, Inspector Frank Kelly, was assigned to the case and, moving in secrecy, obtained an order from the attorney-general to exhume Percy's body without even Mary Bell's knowledge. Kelly's idea was to conduct a discreet investigation that would cause no waves. But on his way to Belleville with the exhumation order in his pocket, he stopped at a police station in Scarborough on the outskirts of Toronto to make a phone call— and thereby changed the whole course of the investigation.

"I'm just off to Belleville to dig some fellow up," he told the officers behind the desk, passing the time of day. "Suspected poison case, name of Bell." Sitting around the corner eavesdropping was a tousle-haired young man with the wide-open face of a seminarian. Two hours later Mary Bell answered a ring at her door to find the same fresh-faced youngster standing on her step.

"Mrs. Bell? I'm John MacLean from the *Telegram*. Did you know that the police are exhuming your husband's body?" Soon the boyish, engaging MacLean was nodding sympathetically as Mary vented her anger over "Gestapo" police methods—why, there wouldn't even have been a body to dig up if she'd followed Percy's wishes. He had always wanted to be cremated, she said. "But that's inhumane. I wouldn't do that to a dog. So I buried him respectably. That's much more dignified."

Mrs. Bell's outrage made headlines on the pink front page of the now-defunct Toronto *Telegram* that afternoon, and Kelly realized that the case would from now on be conducted in the full glare of sensational newspaper publicity.

Out at Riverside Cemetery a huddle of reporters stood shivering in the snow as Kelly supervised the raising of Percy's oak box. A bleak wind whipped off the river as police opened the lid and viewed Percy, fitted in his best suit and the shirt and tie Mary had given him for Christmas. Kelly walked over to *Toronto Star* reporter Fred McClement. "He's in perfect shape. Looks just like he's sleeping," he said quietly.

A steady stream of reporters began to arrive at Mary Bell's front door, often to be greeted by a mischeviously grinning MacLean, now firmly entrenched as Mrs. Bell's friend and confidante. The dark-haired Rusty, a well-preserved forty-one, moved out because of the notoriety now attached to the Albert Street house. But to Mary Bell, giving interviews right and left despite her lawyer's warnings, it was as if she'd fallen into a glamourous role.

Exhuming Percy—"Why, that's like digging up flowers in my back yard without asking my permission," she said, chatting to one reporter. "But what a blessing it was that Rusty was here and I was not alone when Percy was so ill. Rusty told me that during Percy's terrible struggles just before he died he might have torn me to pieces if I had to hold him alone." The reporter clucked sympathetically, and it all found its way to the front pages.

Her marriage to Percy, she assured a fatherly Frank Teskey from the *Star,* could only have been made in heaven. "My husband and I were so much in love with each other, I know he would walk from his grave if he knew how things were going for me now. It doesn't matter how young you look," she said, primping her hair ever so slightly, "When you lose a good husband, you lose everything."

She told MacLean (who was quietly reporting all her conversations to Inspector Kelly) that they'd been married for twenty-one years. It was really twenty-eight, but Rusty was within earshot, and she didn't want to appear *too* old. When MacLean's *Telegram* colleague, photographer Madison Sale, admired her pictures in a family photo album, she declared, "Yes, I'm a pretty fair chunk of meat." And she was always eager to examine her pictures in the newspapers even though, with her dark-rimmed glasses, they didn't do credit to her pleasant features.

She had told MacLean that Percy might have taken a heart pill containing strychnine. Then, when the news broke that strychnine had been found to be the cause of Percy's death, she blithely told him that she had indeed purchased strychnine a couple of months before from a local druggist, Archie Boyd, to kill rats that were eating the apples in the basement—and the *Telegram* blossomed with another big black headline.

By the time the police finally arrived to arrest Mary Bell and charge her with murder, she had been tried by headline to a disturbing degree. And still the circus continued: she was in curlers when Kelly arrived at the Albert Street house; but a couple of hours later, as she walked down the path through a crowd of reporters and photographers, there wasn't a hair out of place. "Would you like a good picture of me?" she asked, coyly posing in front of the police car.

The trial attracted large numbers of female spectators of Mary Bell's generation, many of them patiently knitting while they listened to the evidence day after day. Dr. Reg Anderson, discomforted, admitted that following the exhumation of Percy Bell he'd gone back to his textbooks and found that the symptoms he'd encountered earlier in the Albert Street house were those of a classic case of strychnine poisoning.

His testimony of the three breakfast settings, suggesting that Mrs. Bell was expecting Percy down to breakfast the following morning, gave some support to her plea of innocence; but her credibility was thrown into serious doubt when all nineteen of Belleville's other physicians testified that, in spite of Mary's claim that she'd phoned all over for a doctor, none had received any calls from her that night.

Among the spectators there was a cynical assumption, fed by months of newspaper stories, that Mary was guilty. Laughter broke out when druggist Archie Boyd related that he had sold her enough strychnine "to kill all the rats in Belleville." Police witnesses said they had searched Mrs. Bell's spotless home from cellar to attic without finding a sign of strychnine—or of rats.

In the witness box, MacLean said Mrs. Bell had told him at supper one night, "You know Rusty had another widow woman, don't you? She lives in Trenton and is much older than me. There was never anything between Rusty and me." But a procession of friends and relations testified that Mary was at least mildly infatuated with the lodger, and Don "Danny Boy" Smith, a guitar instructor, quoted Percy as saying one night of Mary and Rusty, "Those two have got my nanny, and I am going to do something about it."

Dispelling any notion that Albert had been murdered for insurance money, an insurance company official testified that the Bells had taken out a policy for less than $5,000 on Percy's life in 1953, but it was to cover a mortgage on their house.

One surprise witness, finance company manager David R. Duffy, related that when he called on Mrs. Bell on January 5 she had told him she had given Percy a drink of hot chocolate the night he died. He'd thought her statement odd when he read later that Percy had had nothing to eat or drink after returning home. But police found no sign of cocoa in the Bell home. A pathologist related that he had smelled cocoa or chocolate when the body was opened, but this was accounted for by the fact that Percy had been eating chocolates at Mrs. Jenners's house.

The Crown called seventy witnesses, but time and again what seemed like incontrovertible evidence only led up a blind alley. Defence attorney Ronald Cass, whose relentless questioning of prosecution witnesses had done much to undermine the case against Mrs. Bell, now took his biggest gamble. Realizing that the jury, hearing the many contradictory statements Mary Bell had made, would be unlikely to believe anything Mary said now, he called no witnesses.

Crown attorney Alex Hall, under Cass's battering, seemed to have lost faith in his own case; his summation was weak and unconvincing. Cass, by contrast, hammered away at the fact that the Crown had established no motive for murder; if Mrs. Bell had been having an affair with Rusty Jenners, there was no evidence that Percy, whose sexual abilities had been impaired by an accident, was doing anything about it, said Cass.

"You must not be ill-disposed towards the accused because she told lies or used bad words or might have been guilty of indiscretion with Jenners," he pleaded. And he reminded them, "The last thing Percy requested before his death was the playing of 'Abide With Me' by Rusty Jenners. . . . I suggest that Bell had made up his mind he was going to do away with himself back on December 14 when he said his wife and Jenners were 'getting his nanny' and he was going to do something about it."

Mr. Justice J.C. McRuer summed up the case plainly: "There were only three people in that house—only three hands to administer that strychnine. It was either administered by Jenners or Bell or Mrs. Bell." In the witness box, Jenners, asked point-blank if he had administered the strychnine, had replied, "No, I certainly did not."

In the United States over the last century, a number of women charged on the most convincing evidence with poisoning their husbands had been acquitted by all-male juries unwilling to send a woman to the gallows. One member of the all-male jury that tried Mrs. Bell was to admit afterwards that in her case this too was a consideration.

After four hours of deliberation, the jury returned to announce its verdict: not guilty. "Thank you," Mary Bell told them, and then wept as she embraced her daughter, Mrs. Tiverton, a Crown witness against her. Mrs. Bell left soon afterwards for western Canada, where she married a farmer. She has since returned to Ontario where, her daughter told me, she recently celebrated a very happy twenty-fifth wedding anniversary.

I drove east from Belleville to the graveyard at Napanee in a torrential rainstorm not unlike the storms of Hurricaine Hazel which had battered this shore during Mary Bell's trial. At Riverside Cemetery the superintendent sheltered himself in his truck while he tried to locate Percy's grave on his plot map, then leaped out and dashed down the slope.

"There it is," he said as we stood, both soaked to the skin. The stone bears both Percy and Mary's names, with a space left for the date of her death. And there at the bottom of the stone, just as Percy would have liked it, were engraved the words, 'Abide With Me.'

A Marriage of Inconvenience

The wind keened in the Scotch pines beside the highway as brown skeletons of goldenrods bent and broke under the assault of one of the season's first snowfalls. It was early December and in the semi-tame wilderness around Peterborough, Ontario, nature had closed up shop for the season. The tourists had long since gone, the hunters were few and far between. Every creature with a home had retreated indoors.

Over the sound of the wind that December day in 1973 came the drone of a bus climbing the steady ascent to a point on Highway 115, some twenty kilometres southwest of Peterborough. At the brow of the hill the bus stopped and two people got out, standing for a moment to watch the bus disappear into the blowing snow.

The man beckoned, the woman followed and they crossed the road, passing through a gate into a clearing in the woods. Exchanging few words, they trudged on into the hardwood bush, following a small ravine which led from the highway; they were soon out of sight. Then—

short and sharp as a crackling stick came the sound of a small-bore rifle.

Four shots. Then silence.

As the bus rolled towards Peterborough, at least two people on board mused about the rather odd young couple they had seen. "I never let anybody off on that stretch of highway before," the driver, Richard Giberson, was to recall.

When the dark-complexioned young man with the English accent had asked him to let them off, Giberson had asked if they wanted any particular intersection.

"No, here will do. I know a farmer who lives near here," said the man, indicating the deserted stretch of highway.

Sybil Burnett was on her way from Oshawa to make her regular visit to her daughter. Watching the couple make its way to the front of the bus, she thought: "Must be Greek or East Indian people. Hmm, that poor girl is going to be cold out in the snow with no gloves and nothing on her head."

There was something else Mrs. Burnett remembered: the man, wearing a herringbone overcoat that didn't look at all like hunting gear, was carrying a khaki case containing the unmistakable shape of a gun.

Winter wrapped the woods in silence, the months passed, and at last the warmth of spring began to shrink the crusted snowdrifts. One April morning two girls, Linda Bottrell and Brenda Harvey, both twelve, were making their first excursion through the woods, skirting the piebald patches of old snow, when Linda saw what she first thought was a bear.

The girls stopped, ready to run if it made a move towards them. But it didn't move. They edged closer. In horror they realized they were looking at the raised haunches of a woman wearing brown striped slacks, her face pitched forward and her black hair spread over the dead leaves.

Called immediately to the scene, Detective Inspector Geoff Cooper of the Ontario Provincial Police was initially baffled. There were no signs of identification on or near the body. The clothing and the pathetic contents of the white plastic bag—cheap Persian Melon lipstick, Pond's face cream—bore British labels and price stickers. The woman's gold earrings and bracelets and the profile of the partly decomposed face suggested to Cooper that she had been a gypsy or was perhaps from an Andean country like Peru.

Drawing on his memory of British police techniques used in the Haig acid-bath murders near London in 1949, Cooper, a colourful, unlikely policeman of Portuguese–Welsh background, had the ground around the murder spot taped off in a grid. The soil was carefully dug up, put in marked bags and taken to a police garage where it was dried, sifted by hand, then examined with a metal detector. For eight hours a squad of policemen laboured over the job. By the end they had found three .22 bullet casings in addition to one already found at the scene.

Shrewdly, the murderer had used mushroom bullets, which fragment on impact. But with the undamaged portion of one bullet found in the victim's hip, as well as the four casings discovered at the scene, a ballistics expert would one day be able to identify the murder weapon.

Meanwhile, Cooper had accompanied the stiff, curled-up body, which bore a bullet wound neatly behind the ear, to the morgue in Toronto. His second stroke of luck came as he chatted with a couple of Metro Toronto homicide squad officers while he waited for the results of the autopsy. Come to think of it, they said, one of their colleagues was investigating the disappearance the previous December of an East Indian woman in Toronto. Her husband, who had since left the country, had claimed his wife had fallen out of a boat in Lake Ontario. The missing woman was Ravinder Kali Rai.

Like thousands of immigrant women, Ravinder had come to a place that to her was only a name—Toronto—knowing that it was a cold place but one where, with luck, her husband and children would prosper. For many foreigners, life in their new country remains an unopened book, and apart from intimate friends and family they live out their lives as strangers, isolated by language, commuting to factories on bleak suburban industrial estates.

For Ravinder Kali Rai, brought up in a traditional Indian village, even her husband was to be a stranger to her. He was a suave, smooth-talking westernized man who had discarded his Indian name, Sardara Sing Kali Rai, in favour of the simpler Steve Rye. It was this clash of cultures between an older Eastern way of life—where fathers ruled their families like tyrants, and where sons married the brides picked for them—and Steve Rye's aspirations to be a liberated Westerner that led to Ravinder's death.

It had all seemed promising that day in late 1971 when a man had arrived at Ravinder's village in the state of Punjab and placed ten rupees in her hand to signify that she had found favour as the prospective bride of a man she had never met. Her fiancee, too, had been born in India, but when he was eleven his father, a former officer in the Indian army, had taken his family to Nottingham, England. Steve Rye, apart from his dark good looks, was now as English as roast beef and Yorkshire pudding, enjoying nothing better than a few pints with his mates in the local pub and endless talk about soccer.

The game, in fact, was his passion, and he even tried out for the professional Aston Villa Football Club until a broken ankle put an end to his ambitions. He got a good job testing telephone circuitry, but his best hours were spent touring the pubs and talking soccer with his friend Mike Singh.

"But there was one thing about Steve," said Mike, sitting in the sparsely furnished living room of his home in suburban Toronto. "He was always scared of his father. His dad was a military type, a real disciplinarian. When he was about twenty-one, Steve bought a moped—a little motorcycle. His father told him: 'First I'm going to throw you out, then I'm going to throw your moped out.' So Steve had to get rid of it." Mike's sari-clad, Indian-born wife smiled demurely as she served us tea. "So, you see, when Steve's parents told him it was time for him to get married, he didn't have much choice," said Mike.

And his father certainly didn't want him marrying one of those flashy Indian girls brought up in England—he wanted a sensible, old-fashioned bride from India.

The selection was narrowed down to Ravinder, the niece of an old family friend, Dalip Singh, a bus conductor living not far from Nottingham in Derby. "Steve wasn't really opposed," said Mike as his two children played at his feet. "A middleman said he'd seen her and she was a real beauty. Steve wanted a showpiece, someone he'd be proud to have around."

Steve and his family went to meet the girl at London's Heathrow Airport—although by tradition he wasn't allowed to speak to her. And when he saw her, his heart sank. Ravinder was strongly built with deep-set eyes and big, widely spaced front teeth. "She was a homely girl," admitted Mike. "Steve was very depressed about it." More, her lack of Western sophistication would create a wall between them.

But there was no turning back. He went through with the civil ceremony at the Sikh temple in Derby in November 1972. The young couple lived with Steve's parents, occupying a room of their own. It wasn't long before Ravinder was complaining to her aunt in Derby of her unhappiness.

She was still a virgin, she complained, and Steve insisted on them sleeping in separate beds. He had even beaten her, until Steve's father put a stop to it. During a quarrel, Steve had suggested to his young wife that she should drink kerosene and do away with herself.

Mike, meanwhile, had emigrated to Canada, and was sending home glowing reports about the job prospects. When Mike came home on a visit, Steve decided that he and Ravinder would also move to Canada. Then, he warned her darkly, once he had her beyond the reach of her relatives, he would fix her.

On November 1, 1973, Steve and Mike flew to Toronto with the understanding that Ravinder would come over later. Steve moved in with Mike to his large, one-room basement apartment on Evans Avenue in Etobicoke, a suburb of Toronto. "My wife was over in India, and Steve was always asking me how I could be without her and why didn't I bring her over," Mike recalled.

Steve soon got a job in quality control at the Irwin Toys factory. "Boy, he could talk. That's how he got the job. Everybody liked Steve. I never knew anybody who didn't like him," said his friend. Steve was now working seven days a week, bringing home between $250 and $300 and taking pride in showing Mike how his bank balance was growing. He never mentioned any unhappiness with his wife to Mike, and within a few weeks he sent a message for her to come out to Toronto to join him.

But Steve was not the happy young husband he seemed. A workmate, Frank Kissoon, was to remember Steve asking him one day, "Would you do away with your wife if you stood to make a lot of money? And how would you do it so that the police wouldn't find out? It's not that I'm thinking of doing it," he added. "It's just a friend of mine in England has this problem."

A week before twenty-one-year-old Ravinder was to arrive, Steve had an odd conversation with his foreman, Arthur Buck. The young immigrant had been asking around to see if anyone had a gun for sale, as he wanted to go hunting. Art had a .22 rifle he was willing to sell. "Could it kill somebody?" Steve asked. Well, replied Art, he was always seeing stories in the newspapers about people being killed with .22s. Steve also seemed unusually interested in Art's talk about mushroom bullets that fragment on impact, making the identification of the gun that fired them impossible.

Could he borrow the gun to show a friend before deciding whether to buy it? Steve asked. Sure, said Art, and brought the gun in to work. "I won't need the telescopic sight or the cleaning outfit," said Steve as he took the gun, promising to return it in a few days.

Meanwhile, Dalip Singh and his wife drove Ravinder to the airport on Saturday, December 1 to catch the plane for Toronto. "She was very worried. She didn't talk very much, but in the end she got on the plane," said Dalip.

At Toronto International Airport that Saturday afternoon, she anxiously scanned the crowds looking for her husband's face. Steve hurried forward, greeted her with a show of affection, then carried her bags out to a friend's waiting car. He took her back to the Evans Avenue basement room which Mike had now vacated so they'd have a place of their own. And although landlord Walter Dworak lived upstairs, he never saw the young woman. Until she made her final journey to the wintry woods south of Peterborough, the basement with its double bed, old fridge and stove and worm's-eye view of Dworak's vegetable garden was to be Ravinder's jail.

Mike called by on Sunday, the day after she'd arrived, expecting to see a bustling, excited young couple. Ravinder made him tea, "but she didn't say very much. She seemed very shy," he said.

On Monday and Tuesday Steve went to work, and on Tuesday Ravinder sat down and, in her spiderlike handwriting, put down her troubled thoughts in a letter, written in Punjabi, to her aunt in Derby.

"Dear Auntie," it says in translation. "I would have written you before had I not felt lonely and upset. On Sunday he was home. I kept myself busy putting away my things. But on Monday I felt like a prisoner in the house. I passed Monday and Tuesday in weeping. I feel as if I am a patient with some long and incurable disease." Steve, she wrote, "is pale and looked very weak. Yet he did not say anything to me. At present I am thinking I should take the next flight back."

Wednesday morning Dworak's wife Mary saw the young couple standing across the street waiting for the bus. An hour later, Mike, who was fast asleep at his new room on Hallmark Avenue after working the night shift at his General Motors diesel mechanic job, was surprised and a little annoyed when Steve and Ravinder woke him up.

He had brought over some mail for him, said Steve. He explained that he was taking Ravinder down to Irwin Toys to see if he could get her a job. After they'd left, Mike was mildly puzzled when he noticed that the postmarks on some of the letters indicated they would have been at Evans Avenue by the previous Sunday—although Steve hadn't given them to him then. After that visit, none of Steve's friends saw Ravinder alive again.

Mary Dworak saw Steve arrive home alone that night at 10:00 or 11:00 P.M. "Where is your wife?" she asked.

"She went to visit friends in Hamilton," he replied.

On Thursday Art Buck was making up the time sheets when he looked up and saw Steve, who had not been at work for a couple of days. The young immigrant pulled the gun out from beneath his grey herringbone topcoat and handed it over. Art, noticing Steve had tears in his eyes, asked, "What's the matter?"

"My father and mother were killed in a car accident on the road from London to Nottingham," he said, telling Art he had to go home to England in the next few days.

Art, checking the gun over after Steve had left, was surprised to find a live bullet in the magazine. He fired it against a concrete wall as a safety measure.

The same evening, Mike, at work at the GMC truck centre, got a call that Steve was in the reception area waiting to see him. His young friend was in tears. "Ravinder is dead," he said.

Sobbing, he told Mike that he'd taken Ravinder for the job interview and she'd been given a job. Afterwards, by way of celebration, they'd rented a motorboat and gone out for a long ride on Lake Ontario. (Mike to this day wonders how he could have been so foolish as to accept the unlikely notion that anyone would take a boat ride on the lake in chilly December.)

He'd been sitting up front operating the boat, and Ravinder had been sitting in the rear. He called for her to come forward; the next thing he knew, a harbour police boat had stopped him to say she'd fallen overboard. The police had searched the lake, even calling in helicopters, but had not found her body.

"If she died yesterday, why didn't you come to see me until today?" asked Mike.

"I was waiting to see if they found the body," replied Steve.

Mike got permission to leave work and took his young friend home. On the way, recalled Mike, "he pleaded with me to phone his parents and break the news and to tell them I was there when it happened."

"They will never forgive me if they hear I was on my own with her when it happened," Steve said. "They loved her. But if you tell them we were all together, it will comfort them because you are very much respected in my parents' eyes."

Finally, Mike picked up the phone and called Steve's parents. His father answered. "I have terrible news for you. An accident has happened, and Steve's wife has died," he said.

There was a long silence on the other end of the line. Then came the question Mike had dreaded. "Were you there?" asked Steve's father.

"It just came," Mike remembers, his hands clenching and his eyes watering. "I said, 'Yes.' It was a terrible moment for me. It was the first lie, and it led to so many others."

On Saturday, when Mike and some friends took Steve to the airport, Steve was again very tearful and begged Mike to write a letter to his mother and father saying it had been a fine day and that they'd all gone boating together when the accident happened.

"Don't worry," Mike told him as he went through security, "I'll write the letter."

"I think now I must have been stupid. But the way he was crying, I felt sorry for him," said Mike.

In Nottingham, Steve, pretending to be overcome with grief, told the assembled families that he would explain just once, and that he would not answer any questions. Then he launched into his fanciful account of the boat ride on Lake Ontario, embellishing it this time, saying that the helicopters had lowered cameras into the water to search for the body. But he didn't enjoy staying around under a cloud of suspicion, so he was soon travelling again, going first to India, then Paris and, in the spring, cockily returning to Canada where he went to stay with his cousin in Surrey, British Columbia.

Steve hadn't reckoned on the persistence of gentle old Dalip Singh, who had gone home convinced his niece had been murdered. Dalip eventually went to his solicitors in Derby, and soon letters from the firm were on their way to Interpol and to the Metro Toronto police asking for more details on Ravinder's disappearance.

By the time Ravinder's body was found in the woods, Metro Toronto police had established that no one had been reported drowned in Lake Ontario around December 5. They had also heard Arthur Buck's story of the borrowed gun and had seized it as possible evidence. Inspector Cooper concentrated his efforts on Mike Singh who, fearing the wrath of his family in England more than any punishment, told several different stories.

He claimed he'd driven Steve and Ravinder in the morning to the toy factory where she'd found a job; he claimed he'd stayed in bed all morning. "Why don't you beat me?" he challenged them, but the officers continued their patient questioning of his conflicting stories.

Mike finally broke down when he was shown colour photographs of the dead Ravinder. Burning with hatred now for his erstwhile friend, he tracked down Steve's phone number in Surrey, British Columbia. With police standing by, he dialed the number. "Hi, Steve," he said, and nodded to the officers. Under the pretext of returning a trunk with Steve's belongings, he got Steve's new address.

An hour later Royal Canadian Mounted Police officers were knocking on the door in Surrey. Cooper was soon on his way to British Columbia. There was, perhaps, a moment of grim satisfaction when Cooper looked at the calm, ice-cold Rye across the table from him, then handed him the two colour photographs, one taken of the body face-down in the ravine, the other of the body face-up and stripped, on the morgue slab.

It was the only time Rye showed emotion. He put his head down, crying and mumbling. "What did you say?"

asked Cooper. "Mr. Cooper, I told you—that is the body of my wife," he replied.

A few days later Dalip Singh flew to Toronto from England on the unhappiest mission in his life. He held the dead woman's jewellery in his hands and tried to control his voice. "Yes, this is Ravinder's ring. Her mother sent it to her from India. And these are her gold bangles. We had them made for her by a Sikh goldsmith in England. . . ."

Cooper had his man, and he had a sound circumstantial case against him. But he had seen too many cases fall apart in his time for want of that extra bit of incontrovertible evidence. The one thing Cooper had not been able to show was how Steve had taken Ravinder to the lonely woods. Two crumpled bus transfers found in Ravinder's frozen handkerchief showed the couple had caught the bus outside their Evans Avenue home early on December 5, but there the trail ended.

A check with Voyageur coach lines finally turned up bus driver Richard Giberson who remembered letting the couple off on the lonely stretch of highway. And a search through the tickets from that trip, incredibly, produced two tickets to Peterborough bearing Steve and Ravinder's fingerprints. Then, answering a public appeal by the police, Sybil Burnett came forward to testify that she remembered the man she'd seen carrying a gun.

During the trial, Steve claimed that while they were out hunting, his wife had told him she was pregnant by another man, and that he had blacked out. When he came to, he claimed, she was lying dead at his feet. But the autopsy report showed no sign of pregnancy.

Rye was convicted of non-capital murder and given a life sentence. "He was a cold and callous killer," says Cooper.

After it was over, Dalip Singh came over and shook Cooper's hand. "In my village today, you are a most celebrated man," he said.

Steve's parents returned to India leaving no address. "His father is a broken man, disgraced," said a friend.

As for Mike: "I've learned my lesson. It all started with

that first lie I told for a friend. After that I had to keep lying. Now I trust no one—never again. But I don't blame Steve so much now," he added. "I blame his parents. He should have left his wife if he didn't love her. Lots of other men do after an arranged marriage. But he was afraid of his father."

How Anti-Semitism
Saved a Toronto Killer

It was getting dark as the three men met on the Strachan Avenue bridge, and the sky was lit by fitful flashes of lightning. That spring night in 1912, Good Friday was being observed in Toronto's powerful Christian churches. For the Jewish population, many newly arrived from Eastern Europe, it was the time of Passover.

But the three men—a slight young Irishman and two middle-aged Jewish scrap iron dealers—had more earthly matters in mind: they were there to make a deal.

The two dealers little suspected it, but the price they would pay for their deal would be high: before the night was out, one would lie dead and the other so badly beaten he would never fully recover. The attack on Joseph Rosenthal and Eli Dunkelman is an almost forgotten but highly intriguing episode in Canada's history.

It was not a question of who did it—Charles Gibson, the nineteen-year-old youth with whom the two men had their meeting on the bridge, was clearly the perpetrator of the crime. Rather, we must ask why 60,000 people, a good chunk of Toronto's population in those days, petitioned the federal cabinet to spare Gibson's life.

Faced with threats of riots in Toronto if Gibson was hanged, the government of Sir Robert Borden finally capitulated and spared Gibson. And after studying the documents and contemporary accounts available, I am convinced that one thing saved the life of this vicious killer—a subtle but forceful strain of anti-Semitism that reached a peak in Toronto around the time of the First World War.

Rosenthal and Dunkelman operated their small-scale scrap metal business in Toronto's old St. John's Ward, a downtown section that now contains some of the city's most spectacular mirrored office towers, but once was a slum accommodating thousands of the recently arrived Jewish immigrants. Rosenthal earned extra money working as a part-time interpreter at Toronto General Hospital. Dunkelman had come to Toronto from Poland with a stopover for some years in New York. Just two years before the attack, his son David had opened a cut-rate men's suit factory on Adelaide Street West which was to grow into the mighty Tip Top Tailors chain.

Our story begins in Easter week when a smart-looking young fellow called at Annie Caplan's second-hand store on York Street enquiring for Rosenthal. "Tell him Smith is looking for him," he said as he left. The same young man called at Dunkelman's shop on Richmond Street West asking for Rosenthal, against using the name Smith. In the evening he even called at Dunkelman's house and left a note for Rosenthal signed "Smith."

Eventually Smith—in fact Charles Gibson, formerly an Ontario Hydro timekeeper, but now unemployed—caught up with Rosenthal. On Thursday night Rosenthal and Dunkelman met Gibson on the Strachan Avenue bridge to discuss a load of scrap metal the manager of the hydro yard beside the bridge wanted to sell. It was to be a "strictly cash" deal, and the three agreed to meet at the same spot the following night when Rosenthal and Dunkelman would bring along a payment of $60. Gibson explained that the deal had to be arranged in the evening because the yard manager was too busy to see them during the day.

When they met the next night, Gibson, according to Dunkelman, wanted only one of them to go into the hydro yard with him to see the scrap because the manager did not want to deal with two men. So Dunkelman took out the $60 he had withdrawn from the bank that afternoon, handed $15 of it to Rosenthal, and watched the two men walk down the bridge towards the yard.

As he waited for what seemed to be half an hour, Dunkelman noticed soldiers walking to and from Stanley Barracks at the foot of Strachan. Finally, Gibson, showing no sign of discomposure, came back alone, telling him Rosenthal would soon be through and that he should now come down to the yard. Dunkelman was to testify that Gibson showed him some rolls of scrap wire and then took him behind the building near a door where, Gibson said, Rosenthal would emerge when the deal was completed.

"Gibson was standing behind me," said Dunkelman. "He said, 'Look at the lightning!' I looked up and I saw the lightning and was struck on the forehead." Dunkelman clutched at a packing case, then crumpled to the ground. When he came to, it was dawn and he was lying in the mud of the hydro yard. He put his hand to his head and found it covered in blood, so he took out a handkerchief. As he felt around, his hand closed on a hammer. It was bloodstained and was obviously the weapon used to attack him.

After a time Dunkelman managed to get to his feet and staggered back towards the bridge. To two hydro workers who saw him he could only mumble, "Me fall, me fall." He was helped home, and his wife Leah was horrified when she opened the door and found her husband bleeding and incoherent. From his delirious ramblings, it seemed that three men had attacked him, and this explanation, published in the newspapers, was to add confusion to the case.

Meanwhile, hydro employees had discovered Rosenthal's body about ten metres from where Dunkelman had fallen, hidden by a pile of crates. A five-kilogram (ten-pound) chunk of concrete had been used to fracture his skull and still lay on his head; a rope had been tied tightly around his neck. Amazingly, the autopsy was to show that these assaults were not the cause of his death. The left side of his chest from the fifth rib down had been smashed. "He died a slow death, perhaps taking three or four hours to die," said the pathologist, Dr. Arthur Jukes Johnson. Cause of death: internal haemorrhaging.

The description of the murder scene, carefully noted by Chief Justice Sir William Mulock when the case came to trial, sounds like that of a blood-spattered slaughter house. The reason for the assaults was not hard to find: both Rosenthal and Dunkelman's pockets had been turned inside out or cut open, the $60 stolen. For Rosenthal, as for Dunkelman, the attack must have come when least expected. When his body was found, he was still clenching a handful of tobacco as though he had been in the act of rolling a cigarette.

Dunkelman, part of whose brain was exposed in the attack, was able to give police little help at first, and his memory only gradually returned during a four-week stay in hospital.

Police, meanwhile, were having little success in tracking the mysterious Smith. But a police detective, carrying out a routine investigation of thefts of scrap material from the hydro yard, pulled open a washroom door on the premises and found Gibson cowering inside. Taken in for questioning, Gibson was quickly identified by witnesses as Smith. At his lodgings at 288 Church Street, his landlady, Mrs. Bertha Jones, reported that Gibson, using the name Martin, had rented the room the day after the murder, paying two weeks in advance.

The same day he had gone on a shopping spree, buying a new suit at Eatons for $15, a baseball bat and various other goods. But what interested police most was a set of overalls belonging to Gibson with a long bloodstain down one leg. His overcoat also bore spots of blood.

At the Ontario Street home of Gibson's father and step-mother, police made more interesting finds: a clothesline on the roof had recently been removed, but police found a small piece of line still attached to a nail, and a fibres expert was to testify that it was identical to the rope found around Rosenthal's neck. The son of the landlady, William Britt, told police Gibson had returned there Friday night and he'd noticed that the young man's boots were muddy. The next morning he'd seen Gibson furiously brushing his pants.

Later that Saturday, Gibson had sent his stepmother, Mrs. Julia Gibson, an odd letter from Union Station saying he was leaving for Sudbury where he'd just been offered a job. In fact, he was moving only a few blocks to the Jones's roominghouse.

For most of this, Gibson claimed to have an explanation. He had run into two men, one named "Red" Wilson, heavily built with a reddish complexion, the other named Alec, short and thickset, who wanted him to contact Rosenthal about making a deal on the scrap metal. Acting for them, he had used the name Smith and arranged the Friday night meeting on the bridge. At that time he had left Alec and Red with the two dealers on the bridge and had gone home, having something to eat on the way, he said. The following day Alec and Red had given him his share of the money for arranging the deal—$40—an obvious inven-tion to account for his recent purchases.

The bloodstain? Gibson explained that on Saturday after-noon his twelve-year-old brother Willie had fallen off his bicycle and had come in bleeding from the head. He had cradled Willie's head on his lap while he bathed the wound, Gibson said. Little Willie duly testified to the incident in court, remembering that his brother had called him a "little son-of-a-gun" when he noticed the blood had dripped on his pants. Mrs. Gibson, explaining the blood on the over-coat, said the coat had been thrown over a chair and that she had casually put her hand on it after touching Willie's bleeding head. The only problem: both William Britt and his mother testified that Charles had been upstairs when Willie came running in with his cut, and that he did not even see the lad before he was taken off to hospital to have his wound treated.

Gibson still might have been cleared. At his trial, the three soldiers who had been in the vicinity of Stanley Barracks said it was their impression they'd seen more than three men in the group standing on the bridge that night. But by the time of the trial, Dunkelman's memory had returned (although a member of his family told me he never fully recovered all his faculties). There was *no* "Red" Wilson and *no* Alec, he said. He turned dramatically and stared directly at the slim youth with the slightly petulant lips. It was Gibson who took Rosenthal into the yard and who later attacked him. "I am positive. I will tell him right to his eyes," he said.

Summing up, white-bearded Sir William Mulock, long a Liberal power-broker in Toronto, told the jury, "If you believe Dunkelman, then your problem is largely solved." But, he pointed out, Dunkelman had no reason to send Gibson to the gallows if he were not in fact his assailant.

In Sir William's bench book for the period, discovered among hundreds of uncatalogued judges' documents in the basement of the historic Osgoode Hall law courts, I found heavy scrawls and underlinings alongside Gibson's evidence with notes pointing out how Gibson contradicted the evidence of first one witness and then another.

Lawyer Aubrey Bond put up a spirited defence for Gibson, arguing that because Dunkelman's evidence concerned his own attack he could not testify in the Rosenthal murder case. At the conclusion of the trial in November 1912, Gibson was found guilty; but Sir William postponed sentence until Bond could make his legal argument on Dunkelman's testimony to a higher court. By the May assizes, the court had ruled against Bond, and Sir William noted tersely in his bench book, "The sentence of the court

in this case is that the prisoner, Charles Gibson, be executed on Wednesday, 9 July 1913."

At this point local establishment wheels started to turn
for Gibson. An influential lawyer, T. Herbert Lennox, KC,
became involved in his case and, with charges that the
police had failed to attempt to track down the mysterious
"Red" and Alec, we find the execution postponed to
October 9, 1913.

"Gibson did not murder Rosenthal," Lennox stated cate-
gorically. "Nor was he present at the time he was murdered. If Gibson dies on the scaffold, it will be one of the
most terrible instances of a miscarriage of justice in history." But the federal government, after reviewing the facts
of the case, on October 1 refused Gibson's final plea for
clemency or a new trial.

"Thank God my father is avenged," Harry Rosenthal, the
son of the dead man was quoted as saying. "I am very sorry
for the young man, but I did object to him getting a new
trial."

The Reverend John McNeil, who had been involved in
the campaign to save Gibson, broke the news to him in the
Don Jail death cells October 1. "He laid his head on his
arms and cried," reported the clergyman. "He was completely broken down and could say nothing." Then McNeil
made a statement that was to make all the difference: "If
the Jews would circulate a petition for the commutation of
the sentence, it would be a fine and kindly thing to do," he
said. "That seems all that can be done for him now."

To understand what happened next and why this statement amounted to social blackmail, it's necessary to know
what was happening to the Jews in Toronto at this time. In
the previous century, German and British Jewish immigrants, clustering around Holy Blossom Temple, had been
able to win a measure of acceptance from the Christian
population. They were still systematically excluded from
social and sports clubs, but acknowledged Jewish spokes-
men usually got a fair hearing.

But towards the end of the nineteenth century and in the

first decade of the twentieth century, with the arrival of thousands of Eastern European Jews, many of them destitute, that situation began to change. Stephen A. Speisman, author of *The Jews of Toronto, A History to 1937,* told me that many of the newcomers, having little capital, went into the salvage trades or became peddlers. As rag-pickers, bottle-washers or small-time scrap metal dealers crowded into slum tenements in St. John's Ward, they aroused much more hostility than the predominately middle-class Jews of Holy Blossom Temple. Anti-Jewish feeling was aggravated by the *Evening Telegram* to the point that Jewish leaders in 1913 asked its editor, John Ross Robertson, to take a more positive attitude towards the Jewish community.

Jewish peddlers canvassing the non-Jewish areas of the city were attacked, sometimes dragged from their carts and beaten, or had garbage or stones thrown at them. A report in the *Jewish Times* of the period appealed to readers to direct Jewish newcomers away from peddling because the Jewish population had become so identified with the trade that Gentile mothers would tell their children, "Hush, hush, or I will call the Jewish peddler." Immigrants should go into "less degrading occupations," the writer urged.

As the acknowledged spokesman of the Jewish community, Rabbi Solomon Jacobs of Holy Blossom had a particularly slippery path to walk during this tempestuous period. It was important for the rabbi to stand up to injustices meted out to Jews, but equally important to the British-born rabbi was the need to win acceptance for Jews from the rest of the community.

There are no records of the conversations that took place among Jewish leaders in the day or two following McNeil's appeal to them, but it's not hard to imagine the response.

Most non-Jews seemed to have forgotten the brutality of the attack on the two scrap dealers, and attention was now focused on the tender age of the condemned man. The hard facts of the trial had been forgotten in the year that had passed, and people were willing to believe there was doubt about Gibson's guilt.

By insisting on "a life for a life," the Jewish leaders reasoned, they would be exposing the community to Gentile anger. If Gibson had murdered a pillar of the Gentile community, he might have been strung up without a second thought. But for attacking two middle-aged Jewish scrap dealers. . . . Justice would be put aside for the present, the Jewish leaders decided—mercy would prevail.

So on October 4 we find Jacob Cohen, JP, quoted in the *Telegram:* "All the influential and best of Toronto's Jews" would sign petitions to save Gibson's life. "It's a human plea. It's not a case of either Jew or Gentile," he said. Then came the final persuasion: Harry Rosenthal, so relieved a few days before to see his father avenged, wrote the following to the minister of justice in Ottawa: "As the son of the late Joseph Rosenthal who was murdered by Charles Gibson in April, 1912, in this city, I request that you show . . . clemency to Charles Gibson, the slayer of my father. Firmly as I am convinced that he is guilty, I, in accordance with and following the teachings of the Hebrew religion to show mercy to others, sincerely request that you use your power as Minister . . . to commute his sentence to that of life imprisonment. . . ."

Reading the letter again, with its assertions of Gibson's guilt, it's obvious that the appeal had to be wrung from Rosenthal, who had little patience with those who, like the lawyer Lennox, were now arguing that Gibson had been terribly wronged.

Meeting at the YMCA, the Toronto Ministerial Association endorsed a petition calling for the commutation of Gibson's sentence, and copies of the petition were distributed for signatures everywhere from the Upper Canada Tract Society to Child's restaurant, with people fighting for a chance to endorse it at City Hall. On the following weekend, there was hardly a church in Toronto that did not post copies for signatures.

On Monday, Lennox was full of thunder as he headed for Ottawa with the petition, warning, "There will be riots in Toronto if Gibson is hanged." With Lennox went Rabbi

Jacobs, who declared: "I am here to represent the Jewish people. I have personally signed the petition. Gibson is a very young man, in fact he is only a boy, and I don't believe he went out to the rendezvous with the intent to commit murder." It was estimated that 5,000 of the 60,000 names on the petition were Jewish.

In Toronto the newspapers performed extraordinary contortions to show that Gibson's life should be spared for reasons other than those in a lot of minds. The *Telegram* argued that Gibson had not received a fair trial because his family was poor and could not afford proper legal representation. The *Star* editorialized that the move to save Gibson only indicated that up-to-date Toronto people were now opposed to capital punishment—although the Toronto public happily saw murderers sent to the gallows for many decades after. The *Telegram* in particular wrote heart-wrenching stories, quoting Gibson's parents and publishing pathetic letters from the condemned man.

In Ottawa, Lennox and his deputation argued for days with Prime Minister Sir Robert Borden and members of his cabinet. Finally worn down, the cabinet agreed to commute Gibson's sentence to life imprisonment, making it clear that the government had no doubts about his guilt. Lennox joyfully announced that the way had now been opened, not only for saving Gibson's life, but to track down "Red" Wilson and Alec and to get a new trial. In fact, said Lennox, he even had the names and addresses of the two men in his office.

At Toronto's Union Station, hundreds crowded around to see Gibson as he was taken aboard a train on his way to Kingston penitentiary. Gradually the talk of a new trial faded. In the general spirit of relief there was only one sour note: the hangman, cheated of what would have been his 307th victim, called it "a travesty of justice."

Gibson's story has an ironic ending. On June 22, 1920, he was released from Kingston penitentiary suffering from consumption. A month later his stepmother, as she told reporters afterwards, went to him as he lay on his deathbed at home. "Charlie," she said, "You are home with your family now, nothing can hurt you. Tell your mother, did you do this thing for which they sent you to prison?"

Charlie looked up with tears in his eyes and said, "Mother, I am innocent. I know no more about how Rosenthal was murdered than you do. There were four of them together. The only solution of which I can think is that they got to fighting amongst themselves."

At least that's the way his stepmother told it, and who would want to doubt a mother's word?

What the Children Saw

"Reckon," said Art Kendall, jabbing at his pork chop with the knife, "that we might all take a holiday next week up the Bruce. What do you say, Mother?"

"Oh, Art, can we?" said his wife Helen, her face lighting up. "We ain't been away in donkey's years. The kids'll just love it."

"Dad, Dad," piped up five-year-old Jean, "is there water for swimming in?"

"Reckon so," said Kendall, a stern man on whose face time and weather had etched deep lines. "But I can't go galavantin' around with you, mind. I'll have to be workin' up there at the sawmill. Somebody's got to pay the bills around here." But their father's glum face did nothing to quell the excitement of the five Kendall children as they spent the rest of the supper hour chattering happily about their holiday in the Bruce Peninsula. "But Mom," wailed Margaret, who was eleven that summer of 1952, "we haven't got any bathing suits. How can we go?"

"Well, then, I'll just find some material after supper, and we'll make some," said her mother. "Simple as that." Helen

Kendall was known throughout the Monkton district of southwest Ontario for her resourcefulness. Old Art, forty-two and nine years her senior, might be a sourpuss, but Helen made up for it by always looking on the bright side. She hadn't complained once when Art had announced that, with the flax planted and nothing else to do around the farm, he'd go up to Johnston Harbour on the Bruce Peninsula to work at Ashford Pedwell's sawmill. Although this left her home alone with the children, she was just happy to see his old Ford turn in at the farm gate Friday nights when he came home for the weekend.

On Sunday the youngsters were up at daybreak, running around and putting their things in the car. The girls, Margaret, Jean and eight-year-old Ann, had been packing their things all day Saturday.

"Now you just sit still for a minute and eat your breakfast, Jim," his mother told their oldest, who was twelve. "We can't afford to be stopping at restaurants on the way."

Even Art seemed to come out of his usual dour self as they drove north with the children talking about the fish they'd catch and the rocks they'd climb. "Keep your eyes skinned," he told them with a wink at Helen. "This is bear and rattler country." And they all got on the edge of their seats to see who would spot the first rattlesnake.

The Bruce Peninsula, jutting into Lake Huron, is a spectacular wilderness of rock and pine; sheer cliffs drop into the transparent blue depths of Georgian Bay, making it today a scuba diver and hiker's paradise. In 1952, even at the height of summer, it was only sparsely populated. And as Art Kendall turned the old car down the dusty road leading eight kilometres towards Johnston Harbour, there was not a habitation to be seen.

If Helen Kendall was disappointed at the little tar-paper shack that Art had grandly described as a "cottage," she didn't show it. "Come on," she said, viewing the dirty, bleak interior of the cabin where Art and other sawmill workers had been bunking, "we'll soon have it looking like a picture."

In no time she'd swept the floor, tidied up and had a bunch of black-eyed Susans decorating the table. The children, running back and forth to the blue lake ninety metres down the road, were so happy they wouldn't have noticed if they'd been lodged in a pigsty. They were in and out of the water all day, they scraped up the soil outside the cabin for their own garden, and one day Jim came home a hero with a handsome pike he'd caught. Another day he was busting with pride after his father let him operate the tail-saw at the mill.

At the end of the first week, two fellows from the Monkton area, Gord Neabel and George Hislop, arrived to work at the mill, making the little cottage even more crowded. But extra bunks were built, and Helen used sheets as room dividers in an attempt at privacy.

George Hislop was to recall: "Helen's meals were always something special, and they were always on time. Somehow she was always in a good humour, and I never heard her quarrel with Art. She was such a tidy woman—pillow slips on the pillows, the floor scrubbed, and I can tell you there were no flies around the food in that cabin."

But shadows lurked around this picture of domestic happiness: nearly every evening Art would announce he had to make a trip into town, either for parts for the mill or to take his boss, Pedwell, in to see the doctor. He'd arrive home late, and no parts ever arrived; but if Helen had her suspicions she kept them to herself. Then one night after supper Art said, "How'd you like to come in to Wiarton with me tonight, Jim?" The boy beamed. On the way to town, his father pulled off the road and they put a load of firewood in the trunk.

At Wiarton they drove up to a small house. "Come on in, I want you to meet some folks," said his father. Inside, Jim was surprised to find a red-headed woman and a house full of children who all seemed to know his father. As he hung back shyly, he was amazed to see his normally taciturn father acting in a jovial and quite uncharacteristic way.

"Come over here a minute, Bea, I got somethin' to tell

you," he called to the red-headed woman. Laughing, the woman sat on his knee and as she bent forward to listen he kissed her. Jim felt his face burn; he wanted nothing but to get out of there.

On the way home he sat hunched and silent in the corner of the seat. "Here, you can take a turn driving," said his father as they drove down the bush road near home, trying to jolly him up. Jim slid over and took the wheel, but what would at any other time have been the thrill of his life had suddenly lost its attraction. When he got home he went to bed, saying little to his mother.

Neabel and Hislop could have told stories about Art, but kept quiet to spare Helen's feelings. Like the night when, before the family had come north for their holiday, the three men had gone into Wiarton for some fun. After a bit of horseplay, winks and a few off-colour jokes, they'd taken out some waitresses from the Olympia restaurant. Art had picked Beatrice Hogue, a loud, jolly woman with seven children, who Art seemed to have met somewhere before. "Yes," Art told the waitresses solemnly, "my wife died several years ago in childbirth." All were sympathetic.

After sharing the little cabin with Art, Helen and the children for two weeks, Gord and George decided to head back south to their farms. "I'll drive you home," said Art. "Helen and the kids will be just as glad to stay here." On the way he had a surprise for them: he stopped off in Wiarton and picked up Beatrice and her seven kids.

He dropped the two men off at their homes, then took Bea and her brood back to his farm. As the youngsters ran through the house and out to the barns, eagerly exploring, Bea couldn't help poking around as well. "Hey, Art, what's these?" she said, rifling through Helen's few dresses in the bedroom closet. "They're my mother's," he said lamely. She looked at him sceptically.

Later on he called on a neighbouring farmer, Martin Barker, obviously with something on his mind. "How's the crops?" he began, although it wasn't long before he got to the point. "To tell you the truth, I'm in the same sort of pickle you are, Martin," he said. "My wife's walked out on me. I got home to the cottage from Tobermory the other night, and there was a man leaving from the front door as I was going in the back door [Martin was not to know the cabin had only one door]. It shook me, I can tell you. Then Helen took off after him."

But in the next breath he was telling Martin about Bea, "a fine woman, Martin. She'd make you a grand house-keeper." After hearing about Beatrice's circumstances, Martin declined. "She got too many kids," he said.

At Johnston Harbour, Helen was unaware of these happenings. During the long sunny days she'd go out with the children, and in the evenings she'd find an excuse to walk down the road to where Fred and Isobel Charlton had started a small store and boat rental business that summer.

On Wednesday, July 30, she dropped by to borrow a needle and thread and stayed to chat; the next night she came for a can of milk, then walked back up the road with Jim. The following evening Art came in and drank a Coke while the children played ball outside. Later Isobel, driving up the road, thought she saw Helen through the cabin window.

That night as usual the Kendall children went to bed at about 10:00 P.M. Just as it was getting light Saturday morning, Jim, Margaret and Ann were awakened by a noise. After that life was never the same.

* * *

Later that morning Art went to work at the mill as usual. At the end of the day he pinned a note on the office door for Pedwell to find on Monday: "The flax is ready to go and I have family troubles and have to leave. I simply cannot help myself." Kendall had certainly planted a crop of flax, going halves with Martin Barker, but Pedwell would still be puzzled by the note because he knew the flax was nowhere near ready yet.

Late that Saturday afternoon Kendall bundled all the

children into the car and went speeding off to Wiarton, picking up another load of wood for Beatrice along the way. Entering her house, he said, "Beatrice, this is my family." Then, quite at home, he went and shaved, and they sat down to a supper of spaghetti and margarine. The Kendalls stayed in Wiarton until Wednesday while Beatrice recovered from minor surgery on her arm. With the stitches out, Art, Beatrice and the twelve children all squeezed into the car and drove to the Kendall home in Monkton.

A neighbour, farmer Jim Broughton, saw them arrive. He had heard the stories of Art visiting the farm with a red-haired woman and a slew of strange kids, so he drove over to see if everything was all right. As he pulled into the yard, his instincts told him something was wrong. Art, instead of greeting him as usual, just carried on untying the wet bedding from the roof of the car. And where the Kendall children would normally rush out to meet him, they now seemed to be avoiding him, hanging back and finally going into the house. Even Jimmy, who had earned $10 for his holiday by doing chores at the Broughton farm, only said a short, "Hello," and carried on helping his father unload the car. Art made no effort to introduce the red-haired woman and her children. Finally, when the rest had gone indoors, Art blurted out, "My wife has skinned out on me!"

"Helen wouldn't do that!" said Broughton instinctively.

"She left for another man," said Art. On Thursday, he said, he came home after work but no supper was ready. Helen seemed in a bad mood, and he put his arm around her and asked if she would go out with him and the children.

"I said, 'Straighten out for the sake of the kiddies,' and she hit me with a cup," he related. He left in anger and drove to Wiarton, walking the streets until 2:00 A.M. He started for home, but instead went to Tobermory, where he considered driving his car off the dock and killing himself. He finally arrived back at the cabin arount 5:00 A.M. to find Helen gone. He woke Jimmy, who told him his mother had left. He hung around Wiarton and Johnston Harbour for a

Mayor D. Jack MacLean of Sydney, Nova Scotia. Although much respected and admired by the community, his political fortunes had begun to suffer. They ended abruptly when he was indicted for the murder of a voting registrar. (*The Mayor They Charged with Murder*)

"Official" portrait of May Bannister taken shortly after her incarceration in the jail at Moncton, New Brunswick. Despite the mean circumstances of her life and the vicious cruelty of her crime, she nevertheless carried a certain air of magnificence. (*The Case of the Missing Baby*)

Donald Morrison, the gun-slinging cowboy who returned from the ranges of Texas and Montana to his home in Quebec's Eastern Townships. His fight against unjust authority made him an outlaw and a legend amongst the embittered Scottish farmers in the region. (*Shootout at Megantic*)

Steve Rye and the two bus transfers bearing the fingerprints which led to his conviction for the murder of his wife. She was the victim of his rebellion against the cultural traditions of his father. (*A Marriage of Inconvenience*)

Helen Kendall, bouquet in hand, with her husband Arthur on their wedding day. Thirteen years later she died at his hand. There were no flowers.

The dirty tar-paper "cottage" in which the Kendall children watched their mother's murder. *(What the Children Saw)*

Russell Johnson, whose magnificent physique and deranged mind combined to make him one of the most terrifying killers in Canadian history. (*A Strangler So Gentle*)

Partners in horrific crime: (l. to r.) Eino Tillonen, George Skrypnyk, William Schmidt and Tony Skrypnyk, on their way to stand trial for murder. The victim was tortured and burned. (*The Hot Stove Murder*)

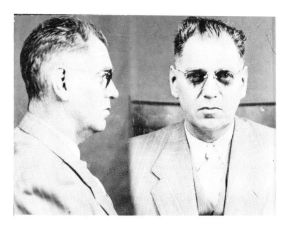

The house in which little Martha McCullough was murdered by her own father (above) and mother. In a delirium of twisted religious zeal, they were convinced that the little girl had the devil in her. (*Martha McCullough: Murdered in the Name of God*)

Keith Latta, former law professor, convicted of murdering a former business partner in Edmonton, Alberta. He is still fighting to prove his innocence. *(The Professor Panicked)*

few days, then asked Beatrice to come and keep house for him, he said.

Broughton shook his head disbelievingly. As he went home, the more he thought about it the less likely it seemed to him that Helen Kendall would have walked out on them: her life revolved around her children. On August 11, when Broughton and neighbour Lloyd Machan called on Kendall to pick up a two-ton truck rack belonging to Machan, Art put on a little display of theatrics for them. He crawled under the rack to help lift it, and Broughton had to yell, "Get out of there, Art. If that rack comes down on you, it will kill you."

"Let it fall," said Art melodramatically. "It doesn't matter a damn anyway. I have nothing to live for. I have $40,000 insurance the kids can collect." Art told Lloyd his wife had left him too, and added that he thought she was with her mother in Brantford.

Broughton decided he'd had enough of Art's stories, and when he got home he phoned Helen's mother and then her brother, Ross Cameron, who farmed the old family homestead in Brantford where Art and Helen had been married on Helen's twentieth birthday. Helen was not there, and they agreed that Broughton would report her as missing to the Ontario Provincial Police. The same evening Ross drove to the Kendall farm. No children rushed out to greet their uncle as they usually did, and Art came out and talked to him in the car without inviting him in.

When the police called by, Art shooed the children away before launching into the familiar story of Helen having left him. She'd taken his $162 earnings from the sawmill, leaving him with only $11, and when he'd come home he'd found she'd also taken some of her clothing from their farmhouse, he said, suggesting that she had returned there after leaving Johnston Harbour.

A nationwide alert for Helen Kendall produced no results. When OPP Inspector Leonard Neil interviewed Jimmy and Margaret (their sisters Ann and Jean kept bursting into tears and could not be questioned), they confirmed their father's story. Margaret told him her mother had thrown a cup of tea in her father's face and, when her father had left, her mother put on a clean dress, packed her nightie and a few other clothes in a brown bag and told them, "I'll never be back, never."

"I want her found, but I don't care if she comes to live with us. I like my daddy best," she said.

Another young neighbour, Jim Baillie, who had worked with Art at Johnston Harbour, was more forthright than other local people when Art, standing on the porch one night, told him the story of Helen's disappearance.

"Aw, bull!" he said. "Helen would never have walked out through that damned bush road."

On September 3 there was an odd development: a farmer not far from the Kendall place found a box of women's clothing in the bush, and in the bottom was a copy of the *Farmer's Advocate* bearing Kendall's name and address and what looked like bloodstains on the cover. Unfortunately, forensic scientists found the stains so small they were unable to determine if they were human blood. A few days later, when Kendall heard at the Monkton fall fair that police were searching the bush where the box was found, he had Gord Neabel, who had driven the Kendalls to the fair, stop on the way home near the spot where the box had been found. He picked up a shovel concealed by the roadside, but later refused to give police an explanation of his action.

The police were now thoroughly suspicious, and on September 7 Inspector Harold Graham had fourteen policemen and twenty-five civilians search both sides of the Johnston Harbour road its full eight-kilometre length. They found a shallow grave, one and a half metres long, which had been dug halfway along the road, forty-six metres into the bush. The owner of the property said it had appeared about the first week of August, but he had no idea who had dug it.

Meanwhile, life at home had been hellish for the Kendall children. The Perth County Children's Aid Society received complaints; and in January neighbouring farmer Clarence Ronenburg was witness to a vicious attack when Margaret, ignoring her father's orders, called by at the Ronenburg farm on the way home from school. Kendall, happening by, horsewhipped her across the yard. But a charge against him was dismissed in court when Margaret claimed an injury to her arm was caused by a fall on the ice. The Children's Aid Society eventually succeeded in taking charge of the children, but after a year, Kendall, who fancied himself a self-taught lawyer, succeeded in getting them back. "Now no jail can ever hold me!" he said ominously.

The years went by, and Kendall moved his family from place to place, but Graham always kept tabs on them and, whenever they could, OPP officers talked with the children. In 1959 Kendall had his wife declared dead, and three months later he married Beatrice Hogue, who had since been divorced by her husband. By 1961 the three oldest children had left home—Margaret to marry a serviceman, Ann to live with her step-sister, Irene Hogue, and Jim Kendall to work at Exeter.

Margaret recalls now, "Ann was always the spitfire. She wouldn't take the abuse. She always fought back." Finally free of the oppressive Kendall home, Ann went over in her mind again and again the terrible wrong that had been done her mother nine years before. "I want Mother to have a decent burial," she kept telling Irene.

Inspector (later Commissioner) Graham was at a farewell party for a colleague when he got the message that Ann was ready to talk. He left on the instant and drove to Mitchell. There, he sat down opposite Ann, now an attractive eighteen-year-old, and listened in disbelief to the story she had to tell.

Going back in her memory to that Saturday morning in 1952, she said, covering her face with her hand when the telling became too much, "I heard a commotion under our bunk. It woke me up, and I heard my mother cry, 'No, Art, please don't.' My father didn't say anything. I looked down over the edge of the bunk and I saw my father go from the lower bunk and lay a butcher knife on the table. . . . I saw blood on the knife. Margaret was already awake, and she put her hand over my mouth.

"I saw my father. . . ." Her shoulders shook now as the sobs racked her body, and Graham waited for her to resume. "I saw my father grab my mother around her shoulders. She was limp. He dragged her out of the door. There was only a screen door on the cabin. I remember it slammed shut. I remember my mother's feet were dragging on the floor. I saw my father go past the window towards the bridge. I could see him dragging my mother on the road towards the mill."

After about half an hour he returned; the children, feigning sleep, saw him take the bedclothes from the lower bunk and use them to wipe the blood from the floor. Then he bundled them up with the butcher knife in a bag and left again. When he came back he scrubbed the floor—something the children had never seen him do before—then told them to get dressed.

He took Margaret in the car to fetch water and, she was to testify, he stopped at the fork in the road near the quicksands and told her that if anyone asked she was to say her mother had left them Thursday night—the night he had taken Pedwell into town for an injection at the doctor's. She was to say her mother had thrown a cup of tea at him before leaving with her clothes in a shopping bag, swearing never to return.

Graham, although a veteran investigator, found himself shaken by the story. "We had realized the children knew more than they were telling, but we never dreamed they'd witnessed the murder," he told me. But it would need the word of more than one of his children to put the crafty Art Kendall behind bars. After telling her story to the police, Ann phoned her sister Margaret, then living in Winnipeg.

"Margie," she said, struggling to hold back the tears. "I want to talk to you about Mom."

"Yes," said her sister, and her heart gave a bound.

"You know since I was eight years old I wanted to find Mom?"

"Yes."

"I was talking to Inspector Graham from Toronto, and I have told him the truth—all about it," she blurted out.

For a second neither spoke. Then, in a small voice, Margaret said, "I wanted to do this for years, Ann, but I didn't have the guts. Tell the inspector to get in touch with me." The two sisters, the curtain of silence now torn away, talked on the phone for nearly an hour.

Kendall was arrested January 27, 1961, at the air force base in Clinton, Ontario, where he worked, and was lodged in jail in Walkerton. His son Jim, told by the police that his father had been arrested, felt a wave of conflicting emotions. There was relief, a strange sort of compassion—and fear for the two younger Kendall girls who were still living at home.

"I want to see my dad," he told Graham. "He may not have been much of a father to look up to, but he's still my father."

At the jail he was led up to a steel door. A drop bar fell into place with a clang. The door opened and he found himself looking into the narrow, lined face of the man who had held them in ter.or for so long.

"Hello, how are you?" said Jim, wondering how to start.

"Fine."

Jim searched the grim face, the blank eyes. More than anything in the world, he wanted to hear his father say something about that terrible day long ago, to end the years of silence.

"Anything bothering you?" his father asked. "Everybody at home all right?" Jim nodded in agony.

"Do you know if Mother [Beatrice] made arrangements about the mortgage on the place?" Art asked.

The minutes dragged by. They stared at each other, and the words eluded them.

"How are they treating you?"

"Just fine. No complaints," said Art with a small, bitter smile.

"All right. I was just wondering how you were." And all of a sudden the tears were running down Jim's face and he had to get out of there. "I'll be seeing you," he said, and turned and walked out. He has never spoken to his father since. In court, when Jim testified, they did not look at each other.

Helen Kendall's body was never found, and police speculate that Kendall, who was wearing hipwaders when he returned to the cabin the first time, had slipped her body into a spongy lake behind the sawmill, the bottom of which is covered to a depth of three metres with soupy, saturated sawdust. Dropped through the crust of marsh grass on the surface, the body would be trapped forever, says Graham.

But in spite of that, Kendall was convicted and sentenced to death. His sentence was commuted to life imprisonment. He escaped from prison once, turning up in British Columbia, and was finally released in 1975. Now in his seventies, he lives in British Columbia with Beatrice.

Margaret told me, "The longer I was away from home, the more I realized the rest of the world didn't live the way we lived. We were brought up very disciplined—yes sir, no sir, never allowed to speak at the table. When I got away I knew that it could not remain untold forever."

Once, after Beatrice had kept the two small girls in a box all day threatening to give them to the mailman, Margaret had tried to talk to her father about it all, she said, telling him they could manage on their own without Beatrice. But he didn't seem to know what she was talking about. Sometimes she'd lie awake at night thinking about her mother, but she never told a soul. "I didn't even tell my husband." At twenty-two, she had a nervous breakdown.

Jim remembered, "We didn't talk about it, but we used to sing about it. There was a song at that time, 'How far is Heaven, I know my mother's there.' We looked at each other, and we knew what we were thinking."

Why did they keep the secret? The police believed it was

fear of their father, and they were partly right. But psychologists might have divined another reason. "Survival was the thing," Jim said. "I guess it was selfish, but the way I felt right then was that my mother was gone, but I still had my father, for better or for worse. . . . My sisters could not provide for me if he was gone. The police would not put a roof over our head. So I clung to that."

Now, he said, he felt nothing for his father, a void. "But I believe my mother would have forgiven him."

The Sifton Murder

The wrought-iron bed creaked complainingly as she got up, went over to the window and toyed with the muslin curtain. Outside she could see the two dark windmills flailing against the gunmetal sky above the barn.

"All right, maid, I'll marry 'ee," he said, turning over in the bed to face her. "There ain't nobody can say Old Joe Sifton don't play the game by the rules."

"Will you? Will you?" she asked, her face alight as she came towards him. "I'll be a good wife to you. Honest, Joe. And I'll give you a son," she said, pressing his head to her breasts.

"Now, now," he laughed, "there's no need to be making promises ye can't keep. I'll be just as happy if it's a girl."

Thunder rolled in the distance. "My, my, won't this set the tongues wagging," said Joe, looking, for all his white hair, like a mischevious boy. "Oh-ho, there's life in the old goat yet!" he said, skipping out of bed and reaching for his overalls. "But Mary," he said, becoming serious, "I don't care about the gossip. Let them wag. We're going to enjoy ourselves."

"What'll Gerald have to say about it, do you think?" she asked.

"There ain't nothing Gerald can say about it. It ain't none of his business," said Joe somewhat defensively. "Now, my puss, all things considered, I do think it best we get married as soon as we can. We'll go and see Preacher Cooper tomorrow."

The Sifton family that came from Ireland in 1819 to settle in the hamlet of Arva, a few kilometres north of London, Ontario, was to occupy a special place in Canadian history. Sir Clifford Sifton, a cabinet minister in the government of Sir Wilfrid Laurier, built a newspaper empire from the *Winnipeg Free Press* and played a crucial role in the opening up of western Canada to millions of immigrants from all over the world in the early part of this century. To this day the Siftons retain their wealth and much of their power.

But when Old Joe Sifton took a fancy to rosy Mary Mac-Farlane, a twenty-year-old dairymaid who worked on his son Gerald's farm, events were to show that family distinction provided little immunity from the pervasive human traits of lust, greed and violence.

Widowed twice, Old Joe—he had always been called that although he was only fifty-five—had lived for a while on Gerald's well-established farm. But they had disagreements, so Joe set up bachelor quarters in the modest pioneer farmhouse on one of his several farms south of Arva. He still visited Gerald's, and it was there in the spring of 1900 that he spotted Mary, with those beautiful eyes, working the butter with her strong white arms.

Mary was then engaged to a former farmhand at the Sifton place, Martin Morden, and they were to be married in the spring of 1901. But when Old Joe asked her if she wouldn't like to go for a ride in his buggy, Martin was shunted aside: Sifton was, after all, a wealthy farmer, and for all his years he was still a strong, strapping man. The kissing in the buggy soon led to long afternoons in bed at the old farmhouse where the windmills forever churned and squeaked. It was on Thursday, June 27, Mary informed Old Joe that she was pregnant.

Joe realized that the news would be like a thunderbolt to the ill-tempered Gerald who, as things stood, would inherit Old Joe's $18,000 estate. A new heir, and that by a milk-maid courted by his randy old father, would threaten all the grasping son's plans for the future. So Joe kept quiet about his plans as he went out, bought a ring and a marriage licence and made the appointment with the Reverend W.H. Cooper, the Methodist minister at Arva, to wed Mary on the morrow.

But a girl about to be married is about as secretive as a rooster at sunrise. That night as she churned the butter in Gerald's basement dairy, Mary sang gaily: "Where'll the wedding supper be? Way down south by the elm tree, ta-ra-ra-boom-de-ay."

"I never heard you so happy, May," said Andy Ross, one of the farm workers, using their pet name for her. "Now it don't sound to me like you was singing about young Martin."

"Ah, wouldn't you like to know," she said mysteriously.

"Mary!" Gerald called at that moment. "I want to have a talk with you a minute."

A little later Gerald came in, a frown blackening his face. "Don't it beat hell," he said savagely.

"What?" asked the other farm worker, Walter Herbert, a simple-minded lad of twenty-one.

"The governor and May is going to get married tomorrow—he has her knocked up. She's been in the family way for about two months. By God," he said, pounding his fist on the table and rattling the milk bowls. "I'll see he ain't going to have her."

He looked up as if he hadn't noticed the other men were there. "You's boys work at the butter and May will be down in a little while. She feels so bad about it now," he said, going upstairs.

Andy gave Walter a solemn wink. But before they could

say anything, Gerald's wife came in, her face puffy and pouty.

She churned listlessly for a while, then stopped to dab her eyes. "Walter," she said at last. "Go down and tell the preacher I want to see him as soon as he can get here."

Then she fell to crying again. "I can't work," she sobbed. Gerald, coming in at that moment, grabbed her by the back of the neck. "Dammit," he said between clenched teeth, "straighten up. You've got to do it. She's deceived us, but I'll make it right. And she won't get a damned cent of last month's wages," he continued, then left.

"I know where he's gone," his wife said mysteriously.

"Where?" asked Walter innocently.

"Oh, never mind. I'll never tell no living soul," she said, and then added, half to herself, "Ain't it awful to think of it!"

Later the two men working in the cellar heard the bell ring and the sound of Cooper talking to Gerald's wife. At midnight, when they went to the pantry for a bite to eat before going to bed, they heard the preacher and Mrs. Sifton still talking, Mrs. Sifton sometimes crying. But there was no sign of Gerald.

Mary, meanwhile, had met Joe outside and had gone with him in his buggy to visit her mother to get her blessing on their marriage. She stubbornly resisted until Mary at last told her they had to get married, then gave her reluctant approval.

It was 11:00 P.M. when they got back to Gerald's and, like young lovers, they sat in the buggy listening to the night sounds, looking up at the stars and making their plans. Suddenly there was a movement in the shadows. "Who's there?" called Joe. A dark figure sidled up to the buggy and they saw it was Edgar Morden, a second cousin of Martin Morden. "What do you want?" Joe asked.

"I was looking for two of my cattle that strayed," he replied. Then, edging closer, he hissed in Joe's ear, "Your life is in danger. You better get away." Joe jumped back as if he'd been bitten, and Mary began climbing down to go indoors. "If you enter that house," said Morden, shaking his finger like an ancient warlock, "you may never see Mr. Sifton alive again. If you're smart, the two of you will come over to my place tonight—for safety," he said.

Still confused, Joe wheeled the buggy around and, with Morden riding alongside on his bicycle, set off again. "I've got to go to my place first. I have to get money and the ring and licence, for we're being married tomorrow," he said.

"Your life is more important than anything in that house," said Morden. "You could be walking right into a trap."

"But who is threatening my life?" Joe demanded. "Is it Mary's relatives?"

"No, your son," said Morden, and Joe sat in shocked silence.

Joanna Morden made them as welcome as if it were a regular visit. "Mary, my dear, you look tired, and you've got a big day tomorrow," she said, already seeming to know their secret, "Why don't you go upstairs and have a lie down? Here, Joe, let me give you a cup of coffee." As Mary climbed the stairs, she looked back and saw Joe sitting down at the kitchen table with the Mordens. "It's all so strange," she thought to herself. "Like a dream. Nothing fits together."

At 5:00 A.M. she was awakened by Joe gently shaking her shoulder. "Come, my love, 'tis our wedding day," he said, smiling, although she noticed he looked tired. They harnessed the horse and set off for Joe's house. "We'll go to Gerald's and get your clothes after, then we'll get the preacher to marry us at 9:00 this morning. I know we was planning on doing it at 5:00, but I'm thinking the sooner we're hitched the better." She nodded and went to the washbowl to dash cold water on her face.

As the buggy crunched along the deserted early morning roads, Joe wondered if Gerald had broken into his house. "He knows where I keep the key. But I can't believe Gerald would do it himself," he mused. "He'd get someone else to do it." As they walked up the path to the front door, they noticed the key was in the lock, and the door opened to their touch. Joe put his hand out to hold Mary back. Without going in, he shouted, "Hello, anyone there?" Silence.

Cautiously he pushed the door wide open and stepped, cat-light, inside. But the house was empty, so Joe went upstairs to put on his Sunday suit for the wedding. They were upstairs when, half an hour later, a voice boomed, "Hello!"

Mary held her finger to her lips, then edged halfway down the stairs.

"Oh, good morning, Mary," said Gerald. His tone was pleasant enough, but she noticed his eyes were red and his face was pale.

"What do you want?" Joe shouted down.

"I brought back that hay fork. I'm going to put it back in the barn," said Gerald, referring to a large hay container he'd borrowed.

"I don't feel too good. I'm not doing any work today," called Joe.

"It's all right. I brought Walter with me," said Gerald. "He can help me put it up if you'll show us where you want it."

"I'll come to the barn when I've finished dressing," said Joe, and Gerald went off across the yard.

A few minutes later Joe came down wearing his best shirt but no jacket. Mary shook her head, pleading with him not to go.

Joe walked purposefully to the table and handed her a roll of bills. "It's a present," he said with a catch in his voice.

"I've no place to put it," she said, handing it back. The only sound was the squeak of the windmills. Joe took out a new gold watch and a little box containing the wedding ring and handed it to her. His hand, she noticed, was shaking.

"Don't go. Please don't go," she said, the tears stinging her eyes. He swallowed, then turned and went through the door.

She waited, and the minutes seemed like hours. The early morning sun flashed on the windmill blades. "It's my wedding day, and nothing can spoil it," she said to herself. "Nothing." And then she was walking across the yard and her head was full of the sound of hammering.

She stopped. "Just foolish fancy! I must be out of my head," she said and turned back to the house. She stood holding the door knob irresolutely. She looked up, and the blades of the windmill were chopping, chopping the sky.

"Joe," she cried, and ran towards the barn. Before she got there, Walter Herbert burst out of the barn door. "Oh, Mary," he cried, "Mr. Sifton has fallen out of the barn and killed himself."

"Walter," she shrieked with a dreadful certainty. "You did it. You!"

"Oh, no, Mary," he said, shrinking away from her. "Don't say that." He pointed wordlessly to the other end of the barn, then ran back inside.

Joe was lying on his side on the grass beneath the open door of the barn. His head was a mass of blood, and near him lay an axe, it's blade glistening. "Oh, your poor head," she sobbed as she ran to the house to fetch water. By the time she got back, a neighbour, alerted by Walter, was cradling Joe's head on his arm and Gerald had harnessed up a horse and left to get the doctor.

They carried Joe, breathing heavily, into the house and laid him on a couch; when Gerald, crying openly, ushered Dr. William McNeil into the room, the doctor saw right away that the man was dying.

"He was hammering some boards on the barn and he fell," said Gerald.

"I'm not surprised to hear it," said the doctor, who had been called to treat Old Joe in March after he'd fallen off one of his windmills. "He was always a venturesome person."

"My poor father, my poor father," moaned Gerald. "Do

you have anything to relieve his suffering?"

"Yes," replied McNeil. "Morphine. He doesn't need anything else. He's unconscious." Joe stirred on the couch. "Have you anything that could put an end to his suffering? Gerald asked more pointedly. "If you don't, I have, I have some strychnine. If money is any consideration. . . ."

The doctor, looking shocked, put up his hand. "I'll not hear of it," he said. When he left, Dr. McNeil told a neighbour quietly that Gerald was on no account to be left alone with his father; but some time after, when McNeil asked him if he'd given Old Joe anything, Gerald nodded, "Yes, I did."

Cooper, the minister, gloomily contemplating the mysterious ways of a Lord who could turn a joyful wedding day into a day of mourning, wandered around behind the barn while the doctor tended to Old Joe. Idly, he turned over a brick lying on the grass with his foot. He looked thoughtful. Then he turned over another. That was odd—the grass was not depressed or discoloured beneath the bricks, as if they'd just been put there. And another thing, there were two pools of blood some distance apart where Joe had fallen. It was all very strange.

Old Joe died that afternoon. McNeil, who was also coroner, ordered no inquest; death notices appeared in the local papers, and Joe was buried in St. John's churchyard at Arva. That might have been the end of it except that, as Old Joe had truly observed, in the country tongues will wag. And as the rumours grew, McNeil, looking back on the affair, began to wonder if he'd been too hasty. An exhumation and inquest were ordered.

Twenty-five days after he died, Joe Sifton was unearthed in an advanced state of decomposition. The pathologist found he had been in good health—but there were two wounds in his scalp, one at the top, one at the side, and numerous fractures to the skull. Inspector John Wilson Murray, Ontario's one-man murder squad, was called in and had little difficulty discovering a trail leading straight to Gerald Sifton.

James Morden, Martin's brother, said that one night

Gerald came to his house and called him outside. "I'm going to tell you something because I know you won't say anything," he said. "There's hell to pay at our house, and I will give you $1,000 to help me out. I want you to go with me and catch the old man when he's going home and smash his head in with a club. Nobody on top of Christ's earth will know who done it."

He wanted his father killed, he said, because the old man "has been the means of killing two women [his wives] and now he's drugged Mary and got her in trouble." He urged James: "You come down and jump in the house, catch the old man and choke him, and then hang him on a beam in the barn. I'll be coming to fetch a hay rake there in the morning, and I'll find him hanging there. Folks will think it's suicide."

"Your father was always a friend to me," said James, refusing the offer. Trying another tack, Gerald asked where Martin lived.

"I don't know the exact address, but it's on Dundas Street in London," said James. Borrowing a coat belonging to Martin, Gerald then set off for London, arriving there about 1:00 A.M. He was lucky enough to meet a constable who helped him find Martin's roominghouse.

At first Gerald told Martin Morden he just wanted him to come and use his influence to stop Mary from marrying Old Joe. But when Martin heard Mary was pregnant, he said he wanted nothing to do with her. Then Gerald offered him the $1,000 if he would come to Old Joe's place the following morning. "We have set a trap for the old man. It would only take two or three raps on the head with a hammer to finish him." Martin would have none of it.

"Well if one thing doesn't work, another will," said Gerald, producing a vial of white crystals which Martin recognized as strychnine.

At some point that night, Gerald encountered Mrs. McFarlane and told her, "If they are not married now, I will put it so that they will not be married today." After Joe's death he warned her to keep quiet about his threat.

As Inspector Murray followed various leads, he found Gerald had been remarkably free with his offers of bribes. The two Morden brothers, Martin and James, were offered $1,000 between them to keep quiet. And Cooper said Gerald had told him he had given Dr. McNeil a $1,000 promissory note if he would not hold an inquest, a charge the doctor vehemently denied.

To his consternation Gerald discovered that his efforts could have been in vain. The old man had composed a new will—on the night he spent at Edgar Morden's—scratched on butter paper. Under the new will his estate was to be divided three ways with a third going to Gerald, a third to Mary and a third to be divided between Joe's brothers John and Alley.

"I'm going to pay Morden $500 for that will," Gerald told Dr. McNeil.

"Why do that?" said the doctor. "Why don't you sue?" Gerald followed his advice, and there followed one of the most curious aspects of the case: in the subsequent civil suit, a handwriting expert from New York showed that the butter-paper will had been forged from start to finish by Edgar and Joanna Morden. But they stood to gain nothing. Could it be that, having heard of Gerald's threats against Joe's life, they confidently expected Joe to be killed and therefore forged the will the night they played host to Old Joe and Mary simply to extract money from Gerald for it?

At dawn on July 26 Inspector Murray and two officers walked up to Gerald Sifton's home, knocked on the door and, when Sifton appeared, announced that he was being arrested for the murder of his father. A few minutes later Walter Herbert was also arrested. A short stay in jail convinced Herbert to confess, and he sent a message to Crown attorney James Magee saying he wanted to see him. Herbert's confession, even eighty years later, chills the reader.

On the Saturday morning at about 5:30 A.M., said Herbert, he was milking "the tough old cow on the end" when Gerald came up and said, "Walter, I'll tell you something, but for God's sake don't tell a living soul. You've got to come with me to the governor's. I'm going to put up the hay fork for him today, and I'll fix the scaffold up and get him out near the end and I'll give him a blow with the big hammer right in the forehead and I'll drop him off backwards, and then we will swear that he slipped."

"Well," said simple-minded Walter, "It's awful dangerous work."

"You keep it quiet and I'll give you $1,000 anyway," said Gerald.

"Well, I guess I'll have to."

"Yes, you'll have to," said Gerald, and the pact was sealed.

On the way to Joe Sifton's farm, Gerald checked with Cooper to make sure his father had not already been married. At Joe's house, Gerald went inside and then joined Walter in the barn.

"You stay there and take the axe, and when he comes up give him a damned good clout, and if you don't give him it, it will be up with us," said Gerald. "Make sure you give it to him on the right side or give it to him on top of the head."

"Oh, I don't want to do it, Gerald," said Walter, quaking.

"You've got to stay there and do it!"

"If I have to, I'll have to," said Walter, "But I'd rather you would."

"You stay there and do what I tell you," replied Gerald. "Don't hit him with the blade. Give him the broad side because we don't want any cuts on him." Gerald went to the end of the barn and began knocking boards off the top of the barn at the point where he was to say his father had fallen. Joe came out and began to climb the ladder. "I was standing south of the trap door. He did not see me," said Walter. "I hit him as he came up with the broad side of the axe—by the right ear. It was not a hard blow. It just stopped him and his head went sideways, and I caught hold of him and held him. And Gerald came and caught hold of him and pulled him up and struck him twice with the broad side of the axe right on top of his head."

At that point Joe slipped down the ladder, and Walter had

to go down. Between them, they shoved and pulled Joe up through the trap door again. They laid him on the hay, and while Walter hammered off a few boards from the end of the barn, Gerald gathered up the blood-spattered hay, scattered it at the other end of the barn and wiped some of the blood off the axe.

"Then he went back and hit him two or three more," said Walter. Gerald now heaved Joe onto his shoulder to throw him out of the barn. "You want to throw him right on his head, then his neck will be broke," suggested Walter, but Joe had not fallen as they had planned.

Following Gerald's instructions, Walter went down and rearranged the body, laying the axe alongside it and getting a few bricks to scatter around. He also, he admitted, gave Joe a couple more blows with the axe on Gerald's orders, although he claimed they were gentle ones.

Gerald Sifton used every legal ploy to delay the opening of his trial, so it did not begin until September 1901—more than a year after the crime. The main controversy in the trial centred around the medical evidence of a number of doctors, some of whom said Joe's injuries would have been much more severe if he had been battered in the way Herbert suggested, and others who said the injuries were quite inconsistent with injuries that would have been sustained in a fall. Dr. Harvey B. Anderson, a pathologist, produced a skull marked with red and black lines to demonstrate his view that it was "practically impossible" for the wounds to have been caused by a fall.

Summing up, Mr. Justice McMahon said pointedly of Herbert's evidence: "It would be impossible to believe a man would say he was guilty of this offence if he were not, and the only sentence that could be passed on him would be one of death. If you think Herbert guilty, then the strongest possible case is made out against the prisoner [Sifton]," he said. After deliberating for nearly six hours, the jury announced that, nine members supporting conviction and three opposing, they could not agree on a verdict.

Rifling through the dusty court documents from the Sifton case at the University of Western Ontario's D.B. Weldon Library, I came across a letter marked "private" from Crown attorney James Magee written to Inspector Murray two days after the end of the trial. It explains a great deal.

Three of the jurors had been influenced, Magee said, identifying them by name. But nothing more is recorded. Could it be that the power of the Siftons intervened to suppress the investigation? Another year went by before Gerald Sifton went on trial again before Mr. Justice B.B. Britton, who told the jury that for Joe Sifton to have died accidentally after the efforts of his son to arrange his murder would have been "the most singular coincidence that could have happened."

However, after four hours' deliberation the jury again could not agree. At the judge's urging, the jury deliberated another forty-five minutes. When it returned the foreman announced the verdict: "Not guilty." The crowd cheered, and Mrs. Sifton wept and embraced her husband. The judge did not bother to thank the jury, which had voted ten to two for acquittal on its first ballot after retiring. He said brusquely to Sifton: "The jury have taken a merciful view of your case. . . . There being no other charge against you, you are dismissed."

In Toronto, Inspector Murray said angrily, "There are times when the jury system is a farce."

The Crown was now in the embarrassing position of having on its hands a man, Herbert, who had admitted an offence that a jury had ruled never took place. Eventually Herbert was allowed to change his plea to not guilty, the Crown offered no evidence and he went free.

And the child Mary McFarlane was carrying? Herbert testified that Gerald had taken Mary back into his home and "got some stuff for her" to induce an abortion. Gerald had made sure there would be no rival heir to Old Joe's estate.

Along the concession roads around Arva where the drama was played out, farm folk still wink when the trial is mentioned. The conviction has come down over the years that, the second time around too, Sifton money and influence had determined the outcome of the trial.

After the trial, Gerald and his family moved to California, but in the 1930s he came back for a few years to farm on property left him by his uncle, Alley Sifton. "He lived across the road there," said a retired farmer, George Fraleigh, whose family has farmed in this area since 1820. "I bought the farm off him in 1936 for $6,500, and he went back to California. Funny thing. He used to have lights on all over that place at night. Scared, I guess."

A Strangler So Gentle

London, Ontario, is a city that God has smiled upon. Rich, smug and assured, it sits in the centre of one of Canada's most productive farming areas, resting secure on the wealth of the insurance industry that long ago found in London a congenial and conservative home base. Newcomers find the city curiously isolated from the mainstream of the nation's life; in good times or bad, London still seems to prosper, its grey downtown insurance company offices and the characterless stone buildings of the University of Western Ontario somehow shielding it from the storms without.

Equally untroubled is Guelph, 113 kilometres east of London, where the hilltop towers of the Church of Our Lady give a feeling of European continuity, and the famed University of Guelph produces some of the world's outstanding agricultural scientists.

It is ironical, then, that these solid twin cities should, in the 1970s, have produced a man who might have climbed out of the sewers of Paris or haunted the fog-shrouded alleyways of Edwardian England.

Russell Johnson was unique in the annals of crime—a startlingly handsome man with a magnificent physique, highly popular, and successful with women. But when that cold stare came across his face, he became an animal, clambering up the sides of high-rise apartment buildings, pulling himself hand over hand up the balconies with his powerful muscles, using his catlike strength to strangle or smother women in their beds.

When at last he was safely locked away, Johnson left the police and the people of Canada with a lot to worry about: time and time again, while women panicked, this ferocious killer eluded the bureaucratic defences that were supposed to catch his kind. Even more disturbing—in four cases he killed his female victims, most of whom were blondes, so gently and with such a prissy concern about tidying up afterwards, that their deaths were first put down to natural causes. His crimes to some extent left the police, the psychiatric profession and the pathologists with egg on their faces. For a while, he got clean away with murder. And this raises a troublesome question: how often have others succeeded?

The four undetected murders occurred over a ten-month period, and in each case the women had apparently died in their sleep, peaceful as babies, in their apartments. The first of the four was Mary Hicks, an attractive twenty-year-old university student found by her roommate in their ground-floor apartment on London's Talbot Street on October 19, 1973. She was lying in a natural sleeping position with no marks of violence on her; a pillow partly covering her face was not counted significant. The apartment door was closed but not locked, and there was no sign of forced entry. Her death was attributed to suffocation caused by a reaction to prescription drugs.

A month later Alice Ralston, aged forty-two, was found dead in her bed in a basement apartment on Mercer Street in Guelph; again, the body bore no visible signs of violence. Alice Ralston was known to have suffered from hardening of the arteries; this was thought to have caused her death.

Eleanor Hartwick, aged twenty-seven, was found dead in her Westlake Street apartment in London on March 4, 1974, the book she had been reading in bed still beside her hand as if it had fallen there as she dropped off to sleep. Her death was also thought to have been caused by a reaction to prescription drugs.

Even stranger was the case of forty-nine-year-old Doris Brown who, the following August, with her sixteen-year-old daughter sleeping in the next room, was found dead in bed in her second-floor apartment on Edinburgh Road in Guelph. Though a pathologist found abrasions and some blood on her throat and rectum, the police were not called, and the death was put down to pulmonary edema—swollen lungs.

Then a killing occurred which left no doubt: a maniac was on the loose.

On December 30 of that year, Diane Beitz, a strapping, outdoorsy twenty-three-year-old, was just going into her mother's place with her arms full of groceries when her boyfriend, Jim Britton, climbed out of his car with a special gleam in his eye.

"Do you love me?" he blurted.

"Very much," she said, beaming. He had been rehearsing the next line all the way in the car from his home in Milton, Ontario, to Guelph. "Will you accept this from me?" he said all in a rush, and before she'd had time to put down the grocery bags, he was holding her hand in his and fitting on the diamond ring he'd bought that day.

"Give me a big kiss, Jim," she said, throwing her arms around his neck. "I love you very much."

It wasn't precisely a scene from Romeo and Juliet, but Diane and Jim were floating on a rainbow of romance that evening as they ate a lasagna supper at her mother's and then went back to her apartment a few blocks away on Drew Street.

The next morning Jim woke at 5:45 to the smell of breakfast cooking. "Come on, or the toast will be cold," Diane called. The two lovebirds breakfasted together, and then

Jim left for his job as a telephone installer. He did not, he told the police later, notice a brown Buick parked outside the apartment with its engine running.

After work that day, Jim bought a bottle of wine and a case of beer for a New Year's party he and Diane were going to that evening. Arriving back at the apartment, he was surprised to see the place in darkness. He let himself in with his key and called Diane's name a couple of times.

It struck him as strange that Diane's black cat did not rush up to him to rub against his legs as it usually did. He walked into the bedroom and noticed a pile of covers on the bed. "I pushed down on them," he testified later. "I felt something hard. I turned on the light and lifted the pillow. . . ."

Jim Britton turned and ran to the apartment superintendent's to call the police and an ambulance.

At the front door police found one of Diane's slippers, as if she'd stepped out of it as she'd stepped back. The other slipper was near the telephone where, perhaps, she had been struggling to reach for the phone. Furniture had been thrown aside like matchboxes. "She was a strong girl, but tremendous force had been used," said Staff Sergeant George Paterson, the investigating officer.

Diane had been carried to the bedroom and strangled with her own brassiere; it was still knotted around her neck. Then, after death, her hands had been tied behind her back with pantyhose, and Dr. John Hillsdon-Smith, Ontario's director of forensic pathology, was to testify, "I have never seen hands tied quite so tightly."

She had also been sexually attacked after death: police had on their hands a necrophiliac in the mould of John Christie, the notorious British killer who in the early 1950s murdered seven women and had sexual relations with a number of them before burying them beneath the floor and behind walls of his tiny London home.

Three hours after Diane's body was discovered, police searching the apartment for clues found the little black cat hiding under the bed. "It was as if it knew what had happened," said Paterson. The only solid clue police had was that the apartment superintendant happened to look out his window at 3:30 A.M. the previous morning and had seen a brown Buick, its engine running. It had still been there an hour later, and police found a black stain in the snow where the dirt from the exhaust had fallen.

Local newspapers, in all innocence, called it the first murder in Guelph since 1967.

It was only much later, after Russell Johnson had been fingered as the murderer, that police going over their records discovered that at 10:30 the morning of the Beitz murder Johnson had reported to Guelph police that a suitcase of clothing had been stolen from his car while it had been parked overnight outside his father's apartment a few blocks from Diane's apartment.

"Perhaps it was to give himself an alibi," said Paterson, "so that if someone was reported at the murder scene in clothes like his, he could claim it was the thief." In fact, this was one of a series of incidents where Johnson might easily have been apprehended.

Going back to 1969, Johnson, married with one child, had attacked a woman in the Mornington Avenue apartment building where he lived in London. The woman had awakened around 3:00 A.M. to find herself lying on the floor with a man on top of her gripping her throat. She passed out and, as she came to, her roommate returned in time to see a man dashing into the hallway, naked except for a long-sleeved sweater.

Upset over the incident, Johnson had himself admitted to the London Psychiatric Hospital. He was diagnosed as a sex deviate but, said psychiatrist Dr. S.M. Nugent in court later, he seemed "relieved" of his symptoms ten days later and was released. He returned twice as an outpatient, and Nugent noted on Johnson's chart that "he might sexually assault a woman."

"If only the hospital had informed us then," said Paterson. "A lot of lives might have been saved."

But the hospital didn't, and in the months and years that followed at least ten women were attacked—and were lucky enough to live to tell the tale. One typical victim, a woman in London, awoke in her Cleveland Avenue home around 3:45 one morning, thinking she was having a nightmare. It was all too real: her hands were tied behind her back with pantyhose, and she was lying with her feet towards the top of the bed, her head spinning.

When she managed to call the police, they found the bed soaked in blood and the woman's eyes badly swollen—but she had not been sexually assaulted. The victim's eyes, in fact, almost had become Johnson's signature: in case after case women had been choked so badly that blood vessels in their eyes had burst.

But there were few clues. When left undisturbed the strangler would clean up meticulously, tidying the bed and wiping away any fingerprints.

About a year after the Beitz murder, the Guelph police again had Johnson briefly in their hands without realizing who he was. A Guelph woman found a dazed-looking Johnson in her house one day. Luckily, her policeman son was at home; he detained Johnson and put a call in to police headquarters.

Johnson's explanation was that he had been high on marijuana and had wandered into the house by mistake. Paterson still remembers "the cold stare" on Johnson's face. "There's no doubt in my mind that he was there to kill that woman and that she would have been dead if her son wasn't there," he said.

Guelph police had also turned up Johnson's name in a search of Buick owners, but because he lived and worked in London, he had not aroused suspicion. The fact that Johnson's juvenile record, showing a series of sexual offences going back to the age of fourteen, had been destroyed, also delayed his identification.

Now attacks were becoming more frequent and ferocious. In April 1977, Luella Jeanne George, a farm-bred girl typical of thousands who go to London or Guelph from the agricultural hinterland to study or work, was found dead in her top-floor apartment on Grand Avenue in London.

Her apartment and the bed she was found in were neat and tidy, but it was clear she had been strangled. The one small clue: this time the murderer had stolen some jewellery and underwear, and these were found in a garbage can a few blocks away.

The apartment building where Luella George was killed is just across the road from a hospital, and it is in an area where many nurses live. The result, not surprisingly, was panic. Police were inundated with calls from women reporting prowlers, and mailmen and meter readers found themselves objects of suspicion and hostility on their rounds.

The panic was only beginning to subside when, on July 16, twenty-two-year-old Donna Veldboom, an apple-cheeked blonde who worked at a gas bar, was found strangled in bed in her apartment on Orchard Street, about a kilometre from the previous murder site. This time, though, the victim had also been slashed in the chest with a knife.

"He hadn't used a knife before. We knew he was going downhill fast," said Inspector Don Andrews, the London policeman heading a force of forty officers working night and day on the case.

Then, checking a list of the tenants in the building, police noticed that one name, Russell Johnson, coincided with one of the names on the lengthy list of sexual deviants they had been laboriously checking on. Not only that, they found that Johnson had once lived in the Grand Avenue building where Luella George had been murdered, and the garbage can where the jewellery and underwear were found was on the direct route Johnson would have taken to get home to Orchard Street had he indeed killed Luella George.

When Inspector Bob Young checked with Paterson in

Guelph, the incident when Johnson had reported his clothes stolen "stood right out staring at us," said Paterson. The police didn't have enough evidence to arrest him, but to prevent any further killings they put a twenty-four-hour watch on Johnson.

As they went into his background, they found little at first to be suspicious of. "Good ol' Russ," to his many friends, Johnson was a keen weightlifter who worked out at the Central YMCA in London and had worked on and off as a nightclub bouncer. His steady job was as a stock clerk at the Ford plant in nearby Talbotville; the worst that could be said of him there was that he was a slacker who took every chance to avoid work. He was separated from his wife, but had a steady girlfriend named Barb.

But as they peeled away the layers of Johnson's life, a darker story was revealed. One woman, for example, remembered going back to her place with him one night, both of them a bit woozy from drugs and drink. She remembered lying down and seeing a pillow coming down on her face. The next thing she remembered was waking up on her own feeling sick and wondering what had happened.

There was a history of mental illness in Johnson's family, and psychiatrist Dr. R.L. Fleming was to testify in court that his family situation was "probably the most chaotic and disturbed I have seen in a couple of hundred cases."

On July 28, with Johnson about to go on vacation, the police felt they had to act. Inspector Young and Detective Larry Ross walked down the few steps and rapped on the basement apartment door. They heard the lock snap, the shower was turned on. They knocked again. At last the door opened.

Facing them, Russell Johnson, thirty, was not a sight soon forgotten. Six foot one, 190 pounds, a trim figure in jeans and white shirt, biceps bulging, he had the aquiline good looks of a Greek god. Behind him the apartment was as neat as a pin, the floors gleaming.

He asked the police if he could phone his girlfriend and his lawyer and then, said Young, "he came with us . . . just like a pussycat."

At London's police headquarters, everyone was on edge as Johnson was led in. After the massive manhunt, was this unlikely suspect the man they were looking for? If he did not confess, it might be a long and laborious task—perhaps even an impossible one—tying him to the crimes.

But within a few minutes, Johnson was unburdening himself, sobbing and spilling out an incoherent story of uncontrollable impulses that even experienced policemen found spine-chilling.

"I can't seem to control myself," he said. "When that feeling comes over me, I'm lonely. I go for a walk. Sometimes I am driving my car and that feeling comes. I can't help myself. I can't drive it. I stop the car and get out and start walking. And I don't know where I'm going. Time means nothing.

"All of a sudden I am climbing balconies. I have strength way beyond me. I've got no regard for caution or danger. My mind is racing at a terrible speed. I am going hand over hand up the balconies and if I lose my grip it doesn't matter. Or if I grab something and it isn't safe, it doesn't matter. One time I was up fifteen floors. The door was locked. The next day I went by and looked up and shuddered to see where I'd been."

He told police that if he broke into an apartment and found a man and woman sleeping there he would leave, "because I love families. I love children. I don't want to hurt anyone."

Describing the George killing, he tried to put into words the horrible ecstasy he found in committing murder: "I put my hands on her throat and my feeling then is like for hours. It's like when you are playing football; you know the feeling just before you are going to hit the other guy? That feeling that you would just like to kill him or tear him apart. It just lasts for hours. I can't control it. . . . I'm so lonely. I could have that lonely feeling even though there are lots of people around me. I have been getting worse. . . . That feeling is with me more and longer."

He told psychiatrist Dr. Douglas Wickware that after stabbing Donna Veldboom he had tried to get his hand into the wound. He was "about to crawl in so he could be safe and warm."

At his trial in February 1978, a jury of six men and six women heard that it would take Johnson as much as an hour to leave his home as he arranged and rearranged furniture, cleaned dishes, put clothes in precise places and compulsively washed his hands. He left murder scenes spotlessly tidy, "so she [the victim] will not be mad at me." Sometimes, said Dr. Wickware, he would wear petroleum jelly and gloves on the job and at weightlifting to avoid "contamination." All these measures, said the doctor, were barriers Johnson was setting up against his aggressive impulses. But inevitably his compulsions, often triggered by a few drinks, broke through the barriers.

Donna Warner, a neighbour in the Orchard Street apartment building, gave a chilling description of how Johnson looked during one of his spells. Hours after he had killed Donna Veldboom, she was in the hallway when he came out of his apartment carrying a garbage bag.

"He kept looking back at me as he walked down the hall," she said. "He just kept looking at me. I don't know how to explain it. His eyes seemed dark and stern. He made me feel weird the way he glared. He made the hair on my arms stand up."

Johnson was difficult to interview, often telling police he just didn't feel like talking about it any more. But bit by bit the story came out. He remembered that after assaulting Diane Beitz he pulled up the bedclothes and placed the pillow over her head, "to make it right again." The only reason Diane had been picked as a victim was that she lived in the same apartment an old girlfriend of Johnson's had once occupied.

In the George murder, "I knew I was scaling the balcony. At the time I didn't know how high it was, but I knew it was the top floor because I saw you guys [the police] up there the next day. I don't remember going in, but I remember choking her and being on top of her. I remember her scratching me under the left eye. That's why I took her jewellery."

In the Veldboom case, Johnson had had a few drinks at the union hall, arrived home about 1:00 A.M., and was undressing when he was overcome by one of his impulses.

"The next thing I was in Donna's apartment." He let himself in with his plastic time punch card. "Why don't people have better locks?" he entreated police. In the darkness he had lain down on the floor beside her bed. "I was lonely," he explained. She got up, apparently to turn off the fan, "and the next thing I was choking her."

Where did such a monster have his beginnings? Friends who went to St. Joseph's grade school in Guelph with him remembered him only as an over-sized, rather awkward kid who always seemed to be overshadowed by his brighter older brother.

"Every kid in school wanted to fight him. He was so big, but you only had to say boo and he'd collapse," said one former fellow student. "He liked to play basketball, but he just wasn't aggressive." The family lived across from the school, and Johnson's friends remember his mother as "a tired, haggard-looking woman who never went out."

Ed Oliver, a school friend who developed an interest in body building and worked as a club bouncer around London, remembered that in earlier years Russ was famous for never being around when customers cut up rough. "It was a standing joke that he'd always make himself scarce," he said.

But after he went into weightlifting seriously and developed a powerful body, Russ was "readier" to get into a fight, said Ed. By then he was also getting into drugs, and Ed and his wife had a chilling moment one night when Russ and his younger brother came staggering out of a shop doorway, apparently intent on aggression. "Russ had a glassy, distant look on his face. Then he saw it was us, and they just giggled and went on down the street. My wife still shudders when she thinks about it," he said.

Predictably, Johnson was found not guilty by reason of insanity and was committed to the Oak Ridge maximum security wing of the Ontario Mental Health Centre at Penetanguishene. But due to a legal slip-up, the four until-then undiscovered murders were not mentioned before sentencing.

That left police in London and Guelph with four unsolved murders on their books, so they took the highly unconventional step of presenting a dossier on the four murders and ten other assaults Johnson had admitted to at a meeting of the London police commission. Critics in the Ontario Legislature pointed out that this meant Johnson had in fact been found guilty of these crimes without having had a proper defence; but Attorney-General Roy McMurtry backed the London commission, saying it was justified in clearing the docket so that the public would be assured that the man who had committed the crimes "is not still walking the streets."

In his moments of madness, Johnson was truly a monster—perhaps the most frightening killer this country has ever seen. But in his quieter moments, he was just another human being tortured by the knowledge of his guilt. "There have been so many, so many terrible things," he told police.

"Sometimes," said Inspector Andrews, "you feel hard towards someone who has killed someone else. You can't help it. But with Johnson I think we felt sorry for him. He couldn't help himself."

The Hot Stove Murder

In a big city the spot on the sidewalk where a bank robber was shot down at noon goes unnoticed by the crowds scurrying to catch the subway home from work. But in smaller communities like Fort Frances, a pulp and paper town tucked away in the northwest corner of Ontario between the United States and Manitoba borders, it's quite different. Today, nearly forty years after the event, the memory of the Hot Stove Murder clings to this town's tidy, tree-lined streets just as pervasively as the sweet, mortal stench of the Boise Cascade pulp mill down by the river.

The events of a crime so sadistic that it made headlines around the world in 1944 are still too close not to cause pain. At the town's tiny prison, inmates in full public view walk listlessly around a chicken coop of an exercise yard, their feet shuffling over the unmarked graves of three local men who were hanged for that murder. A retired prison guard avoids my questions and then finally blurts out, "I've tried to put it out of my mind all these years. I want to forget it."

In a bungalow on the outskirts of Fort Frances, I spoke to

a woman who remembered the execution day as if it were yesterday. And no wonder: it was the day of her sixteenth birthday, and her dearly loved brother was one of those hanged. As we talked, the sad story emerged—how that crime had blighted his family, creating distance and coldness and a refusal to talk about the past even now, so many years later.

Fort Frances, an isolated spot sitting in the middle of millions of square kilometres of forest and waterway, was more a frontier community in 1944 than it is today. In the austere climate of wartime Canada, its citizens found support in either the stern admonitions of fundamentalist Christianity or the merchandise of the bootleggers. Some young men who through illness or sloth had avoided the armed forces and the defence of their country moved casually back and forth between jobs in the bush, interludes of bootlegging and other petty crimes. It was within this floating group that the Hot Stove Murder was born.

It started with a remark by an unthinking young woman to her boyfriend, but it wasn't until two years later that the crime, like a hidden festering sore, finally burst into public view.

Foreman George Armstrong and the men on his roadbuilding crew were just washing up after quitting time on a cloudy June day at Flanders, ninety-seven kilometres east of Fort Frances along the CN railway track. Suddenly a small boy burst out of the bush, panting and sobbing.

"He was just about beat," remembered Don Christian, who was working on the gang that day. "And he was hollering, 'Somebody's beating up and burning my mom!'"

The men piled into an old truck without a muffler and went roaring along the bush road; but as they pulled up beside the log house standing just a few metres from the CN track, there was an eerie silence. Some of the men rushed inside and found the house in total disorder—mattresses thrown to the floor, dishes smashed, furniture overturned, even sugar from the cannister spilled over the kitchen table. The wood stove, peculiar for a June day, was warm, and the men noticed in horror that pieces of what appeared to be human skin were seared to its surface.

Armstrong, guided by the lad, eight-year-old Arthur Jamieson, had dashed to the root cellar, a sod structure at the back of the house used for storing preserves and root crops. The door was locked; from inside he heard the frightened voice of Arthur's older brother Harold, aged ten.

Today the spot is uninhabited, visited only occasionally by blueberry pickers who often don't notice the few overgrown logs remaining from the Jamieson house. But the men who were there that day in 1944 will never forget what they saw when the root cellar door was broken open.

To go back a few hours, that Saturday had started quietly enough for Viola Jamieson, a petite woman of forty-nine known in the neighbourhood for her splendid preserves and, it was whispered, for selling a little whiskey on the side. She and the two boys had gone in the truck with Isaac Sheldon, her common-law husband, to his workplace thirty-five kilometres away.

Dropping him off, she slid behind the wheel and drove home, calling for a few groceries in Flanders. As Viola Jamieson came out of the store, she somehow didn't feel like going back to the empty house—a couple of weeks earlier, thieves had broken into the root cellar and stolen $1,200 she had buried under a plank, and she still didn't feel quite comfortable and secure about the place. But the boys needed their bath and supper had to be made, so she turned the truck towards home. As she got out, Mrs. Jamieson noticed unfamiliar tracks in the grass. Instinct told her to get back into the truck and go for help, but she shook off her fears as idle fancies, walked up to the door and put the key into the lock.

From the darkness two men lunged towards her, one throwing a sheet over her head. Two other men ran through the door, collared the two Jamieson boys and locked them kicking and fighting into the root cellar. There they listened in terror to their mother's distant screams.

Mrs. Jamieson was thrown to the floor, and one of her assailants put his boot on her throat while they demanded to know where she kept her money. "Torture the son of a bitch!" rasped one of the men who had a sweater pulled up over his head to hide his features.

Ripping back her clothes, the men took turns to hold her while lit newspapers were held to her arms and body. Through her screams she still denied she had any money hidden. Finally the man wearing the sweater walked into the kitchen, stuffed newspaper into the stove, and lit it.

As it heated up, two of them grabbed Mrs. Jamieson, lifted her up and laid her bare back on the top of the stove. The smell of seared flesh filled the little house; at one point one of the men saw the flames licking her arms. Finally her screams, moans and denials became quieter. Frustrated and furious, they lifted her off the stove half unconscious.

"Let's see how much water she can take. We'll put her in the well," said one of her attackers. But two of the others had no stomach for it and, without a word, they lifted her, carried her outside and flung her in the root cellar, slamming the door before the boys could escape. Arthur and Harold tried to console their moaning mother; then the younger lad, forgetting caution, started digging in the soft earth of the wall with his bare hands. Soon there was a hole large enough for Arthur to squeeze his tiny body through.

He stuck out his head; the coast seemed clear, and he wriggled out like a snake. Once on his feet, he ran like lightning for the bush. "Hey, come back, you little bastard!" yelled one of the men who had been across the railway track, and he lumbered after Arthur. Terrified for his life, leaping, dodging and stumbling, the boy darted through the trees, eluding his pursuer. A short time afterwards the men heard the approaching roar of the construction gang truck, and they made off at full speed, circling Flanders on foot, then stealing a rail handcart to make their getaway along the CN track. It was only a few minutes later that George Armstrong, his eyes blinded by daylight, stood peering into the root cellar. Mrs. Jamieson lay partially covered by a sheet, the skin peeled right back from her clenched hands.

As Armstrong tried to lift her, she screamed in agony, and he had to lower her to the ground again. "Her skin was burned off her body. She couldn't stand for anyone to touch her," he said later. Groggy and in terrible pain, she insisted that she would rather walk than face the agony of being lifted, so the men put planks up to the bed of the truck, and she walked up gingerly and lay down on a mattress. At Flanders the women tried to give her first aid while Armstrong made arrangements for the first freight train to be flagged down.

Late that night she was lifted into a caboose, and by the early hours of the morning she was in hospital in Fort Frances where doctors found she had suffered second- and third-degree burns to thirty percent of her body.

She lived for three weeks, although doctors said later that her injuries made death inevitable. Near the end, with a manhunt already underway, she asked to see a Crown attorney. The poignant exchanges, recorded in the microfilm cabinets of the provincial archives, bring Mrs. Jamieson's tragedy to light.

"Do you think you will live?" he asked her.

"It's hard to say," she replied.

"Have you taken the last sacrament yet?"

"No, I am going to take it in a few minutes."

"You fear you are going to die?"

"Yes." Then she told the fearful story of the crime.

"And they put you on the stove and burned you badly? Your stomach, arms and hands were burned badly?" the lawyer concluded.

"Yes," came the almost inaudible voice.

Three days later Mrs. Jamieson was dead.

The case caused outrage in Toronto, the provincial capital, and the province offered a $1,000 reward for the capture of the outlaws.

A "dastardly crime," Ontario Police Commissioner W.H. Stringer called it, dispatching two top Criminal Investigation Branch men, Chief Inspector Albert Ward and Inspector Frank Kelly, to the scene.

It was Mrs. Jamieson's tempting preserves that provided the two policemen with their first and, as it turned out, conclusive piece of evidence. Her attackers, it seemed, had interrupted their search of the house and root cellar to eat lunch, opening several jars of the preserves; both the jars and a coal oil lamp they'd left in the root cellar yielded three beautiful sets of fingerprints.

Their next job was to find out who had been talking about Mrs. Jamieson's hidden hoard of money in the root cellar. They didn't have far to look.

A married daughter of Mrs. Jamieson's, Bernice Casnig, admitted that she told no fewer than three men about her mother's buried money, one of them former boyfriend William Schmidt, aged twenty-eight, the ne'er-do-well son of a highly religious Fort Frances couple who had nine other children. All three men had left town, but police soon tracked down two of them and found they had satisfactory alibis. Of Schmidt there was no sign.

Ward and Kelly pumped local Ontario Provincial Police Constable Bill Parfitt for the names of local troublemakers who might have been involved in the killing, and right at the top of the list he put two Fort Frances brothers, George and Tony Skrypnyk. George, aged twenty-eight, surly when asked where he'd been the day of the attack, said, "I don't see it's any of your business, but I was in Port Arthur with friends."

Their names?

"A family named Tillonen."

And what about twenty-three-year-old Tony Skrypnyk?

"I was there too," he said.

In Port Arthur Mrs. Tillonen remembered the men having been there that day with her nephew.

Then came the break the police had been waiting for. A short, dark-haired man named Percy Davidson stopped Inspector Kelly on the street in Fort Frances. "I can tell you something about that Jamieson murder," he said. At the police station Davidson said that the month before he had followed a couple of fellows to the Horseshoe Cafe for several nights in a row, sitting in the next booth and trying to hear what they were saying. One night, he said, they'd been talking about how seriously a woman had been hurt, and that it was "too bad we left those fingerprints."

"Too bad we didn't burn the shack down," one of them had said.

Who were they?

"George and Tony Skrypnyk and a fellow named Eino something. He's tall and thin and wears glasses," said Davidson. "He's a Finn, I think."

And why, asked the officer, had Davidson been following them? He looked shamefaced. His wife, he said, had been going out with one of the men, and he wanted to get the goods on the philanderer. Kelly quickly identified the third man as Eino Tillonen, aged nineteen, and a further check in Port Arthur showed the three men hadn't arrived at Tillonen's aunt's home until after the murder, at 3:00 or 4:00 in the morning.

But the three men had disappeared just as completely as if they'd never existed. For weeks during the sweltering heat of summer, Ward and Kelly criss-crossed the north, following up on every wisp of a rumour about the whereabouts of their quarry, travelling thousands of kilometres by passenger train, boxcar and even handcart to reach isolated work camps inaccessible by road.

Finally police in Kenora, north of Fort Frances, spotted a tall, thin youth with spectacles answering the description of Tillonen, and the same day the Skrypnyk brothers were picked up in the area. The Skrypnyks sat tight-mouthed and uncooperative as Inspector Ward cautioned them and asked if they wanted to make a statement. But Tillonen, youngest of the gang, cracked right away. "I'll tell you what happened. It was Bill Schmidt's idea," he said.

Schmidt, it turned out, was the key to the affair. For three years the thought of that money buried in the root cellar had preyed on his mind, and time and again he'd tried to persuade the Skrypnyks to join him in going to Flanders to steal the money. Finally in the spring of 1944 the three men had done so, but had only found $1,200—a lot less than they expected.

A few weeks later they got Tillonen to join them in another attempt. Mrs. Jamieson had $20,000 hidden away, Schmidt told the impressionable young Finn, and his share would be $5,000. Tillonen's eyes lit up. "I never had more than $100 in my life," he said.

They jumped a freight car late one night at Port Arthur and headed west. "I know how we can make her talk—torture her with fire," said Bill, and they all laughed a little uncomfortably.

At the deserted Jamieson house, they ripped everything apart in search of the money, but all they found was $40 Mrs. Jamieson had concealed in the sugar cannister that morning. When Mrs. Jamieson came home, Schmidt, well known to the Jamieson family, pulled the sweater over his head as a disguise and, as the unfortunate woman came through the door, pushed the reluctant Tillonen almost on top of her, grappling the sheet over her head. Tillonen claimed he was outside keeping watch while the others burned Mrs. Jamieson.

Meanwhile the police had found another valuable witness to Schmidt's involvement: Pearl Lee, a slim, dark-haired waitress with whom Schmidt had been living, told them he had come home one Sunday and told her, "Pearl, you know I was with the boys at Flanders."

"I gave him $50. We cried as we said good-bye. I watched him go from the bedroom window. He had a little grip in one hand. When he reached the sidewalk, he turned around and waved. Right then I felt I would never see him again," said Pearl.

A description of Schmidt had been circulated to police across the country, and within days of the other three arrests a Royal Canadian Mounted Police officer spotted a man answering the description working on a farm at Morris, forty-eight kilometres south of Winnipeg.

"Schmidt? No, that's not my name. My name's Snyder," said the man, but police were suspicious because the man did not have his required wartime identification papers with him.

A telegram to the OPP brought an officer from Fort Frances who had known Schmidt; when the two met, Schmidt knew the game was up. Like rats struggling to escape a trap, the four men were turning on each other now, each blaming the other for the vicious crime. According to Schmidt's version of the story, it was the Skrypnyk brothers' idea to torture Mrs. Jamieson, and he too claimed he had been outside guarding the two boys when the burning took place.

At the trial in September in Fort Frances, Schmidt tried to assume the cloak of respectability he had discarded so long ago, appearing in court in the neat suit and tie a bank clerk might wear. Defence counsel argued that if Mrs. Jamieson had received proper medical care earlier she might have survived, but when the jury retired there were few who gave much for the chances of the four men.

Only two women had the courage to hope. Schmidt's mother and Pearl Lee went to a nearby Pentecostal church and prayed for two hours while waiting for the verdict. They couldn't bear to return to the courtroom, but when one of Bill's brothers came out crying they didn't need to be told what the verdict was—all four men had been sentenced to hang December 6, although the jury had brought in a recommendation of mercy for Tillonen.

For the friends and families of the men, the verdict was difficult to bear—especially so for the Schmidts. Kindly, God-fearing Herman Schmidt had raised his family strictly by the Bible, but it was if his wayward son Bill had been sent into the world to destroy everything his parents stood for. One snapshot will perhaps tell the story: when he heard I was writing about the Hot Stove Murder, Claude Wagner, who had worked with Schmidt and the Skrypnyks at an iron ore drilling site near Fort Frances prior to 1944, called to share his memories of the murderers.

"Old man Schmidt was working in the camp too, and every break we'd get the old man would sit down by the stove with his Bible. But that Bill, oh boy, he was a bad one," he recalled. "One day I saw him hit the old man on the side of the face and throw the Bible out in the snow. Yes, a bad one."

Old man Schmidt could not be blamed for thinking he was facing the trials of Job. The family lived less than a block from the jail and was forced to watch the gallows going up bit by bit behind a makeshift barricade outside the town jail. Ironically, Schmidt, who worked in a local lumber yard, had unknowingly trimmed the lumber for his son's gallows.

As the structure grew beside the jail, local emotions for and against the killers ran high, and the town council, fearing a riot, asked the attorney-general to have the execution held in Kenora where the four men were imprisoned. The coldly official answer came back that the law required the sentence be carried out in the district where the crime had occurred.

On December 4, the roads icy and almost impassable, a convoy of four police cars set out from Kenora with the four guilty men. After a hair-raising drive, they arrived in Fort Frances to be greeted with the news that Tillonen's death sentence had been commuted to life imprisonment. Then there were three.

At 5:30 P.M., in response to a last-minute bid by Schmidt, a telegram arrived postponing his execution until March 1, allowing him time to appeal to the Supreme Court of Canada. Then there were two.

Pressure at the jail was unbearable. Angry townspeople, concerned that Schmidt might get off while the others hanged, retained ace Toronto lawyer Joseph Sedgwick to seek a stay of execution for the Skrypnyks. In their cells the two brothers prayed and sang hymns. Finally, with only a few hours to go, word arrived that they too had been granted a stay of execution until March 1.

Hunting through case documents at the provincial

archives, I came across the explanation for Schmidt's mysterious stay of execution. Police reports show that he had written to his mother implicating two other people, a man and a woman, as the actual instigators of the Jamieson robbery. In a subsequent statement to police, he claimed the man in question operated a sort of "thieves kitchen" in Port Arthur and had dispatched the men to Flanders with the admonition: "Don't be like kids. You got to do a good job. Some of them you have to torture good."

Inspectors Ward and Kelly hurried back to Fort Frances to check out the new claim. But after careful investigation and a comparison of Schmidt's statement to the other three prisoners' statements, they concluded Schmidt had only made a last-minute ploy to save his neck. His ruse delayed the hangings, but when his appeal was rejected the hangman returned to Fort Frances.

This time, in response to townspeople's complaints, the gallows were built inside the jail. You can see today where the hangman cut a hole in the floor and ceiling of what was then the nurse's room, right next to the bedroom of the jail superintendent's children. Affixing his pulleys to a beam in the jail roof, he then constructed a trap door in the floor (a 634-kilogram metal door dispatched from Sudbury hadn't arrived in time). Where the doomed men would come plummeting down into the prison reception area, he cut a hole through to the basement to ensure they would not cheat death by landing on their feet.

Outside, right alongside the town's bowling green, three graves dug in December had been left open and waiting. As the execution hour approached, a posse of armed OPP officers kept an eye open for trouble. At one point *Toronto Star* photographer Fred Davis posed Bernice Casnig for a photograph in front of the jail. His old-fashioned flashgun went off with a loud retort, and policemen came running out of the jail, weapons drawn.

"Don't shoot! Don't shoot!" yelled Davis, dropping his camera and throwing up his hands.

When midnight arrived the Skrypnyk brothers were hanged, as they had requested, back to back. Half an hour later Schmidt too was executed. "The mistakes are always found out too late," he had written to Pearl Lee from jail. "No shame was ever put on the family or on you until I started going with the wrong company. Don't look down on me too harshly."

But it didn't end there that cold March night. Mrs. Margaret Kruger, William's sister and the only member of the Schmidt family now living in Fort Frances, still worries and wonders how it all happened and why it destroyed them as a family.

"I could never understand it," she said, a worried frown replacing the bright smile she'd greeted me with at the door. "Bill was never a violent person. Perhaps in a different time under different circumstances it would never have happened. He'd tried to get into the army, but he was turned down for medical reasons.

"If jobs hadn't been so hard to get, if it wasn't so hard to get two nickels to rub together, if . . ." Her voice trailed off. "My mom and dad were strong Bible people. They're lying over there now," she said with a nod towards the graveyard across the road. "And I think in the long run it killed my mother. What people never realized was that our family and the Jamiesons were quite close—they used to stay at our place when they came to town. We could never understand it."

Her eyes filled with tears. "And it tore our family apart. There were nine of us left, and soon after all the other kids left Fort Frances. They've never been back—except for Mom and Dad's funerals. They try to wipe it out."

Being German-born during the war hadn't helped either, and a local minister has since written a book accusing her father of Nazi sympathies. "He was the very opposite," said Mrs. Kruger. But the real hurt is still within the family. "We've never been able to talk about it. . . . I wish we could," she said wistfully.

As I left, a large brown bear ambled across the road opposite the Krugers' suburban-style bungalow, a reminder that Fort Frances is still not so far from it's frontier past.

Sifting through the official case documents back in Toronto, I found myself wondering, like Mrs. Kruger, *why* it had happened. There in the documents I found evidence that Mrs. Jamieson, in fact, had another $700 buried under a rock near the house. Had she told her attackers, she might have been spared.

The money was used to pay her hospital bill and funeral expenses.

Martha McCullough:
Murdered in the Name of God

"The temperature this morning . . . a brisk 36 below," said the announcer on radio station CJOB as I parked beside the road in Elmwood cemetery and consulted the map they had given me in the cemetery office. I stepped out into the Winnipeg winter, nostrils freezing, eyes watering from the brilliant sun on the snow, and plodded one step after another through the deep powder towards a group of baby blue and pink plastic wreaths.

No stone marks the grave. Perhaps that is just as well—if the epitaph were forthright, it would state that seven-year-old Martha Louise McCullough was murdered in the name of God.

Religious intolerance and fanaticism run through Canada's history like an old wound. From the law-defying Doukhobors in British Columbia, stripping themselves and burning their homes, to the Roman Catholic repression that stifled Quebec for three centuries; from the venom of the old-time Orange Day parade marchers in Toronto to the stern Mennonites settling like flocks of crows in Ontario and the Prairies, religion has often cast a sombre shadow over this country.

To many, of course, religion brought joy and certainty in an unsettled world; but I remember listening one summer evening to a mechanic in Toronto relating in a flat, unemotional voice how, after his wife had joined the Jehovah's Witnesses, his little home had become a religious battleground, and how the fighting ended only when their thirteen-year-old son, unable to endure any more, went up to his room, secured his belt to the door knob and, without a sound, choked himself to death.

I remember the cheerful, hard-working Hutterites at a colony south of Winnipeg who invited me to dinner, showing me their stark homes and their ultramodern farming operations. And I remember the chill that went down my back as they told me of an eighteen-year-old youngster from the colony who, after going to northern Manitoba to work in a mine in search of adventure, had to stand before the community and apologize to make spiritual restitution on his return.

And I thought now of Martha Louise, a sunny, fair-haired little girl lying beneath the snow beside her daddy and of the strange words, tinged with medieval superstition, that the Reverend H.G. Tolton had uttered over her sadly broken body. "The life of little Martha Louise," he told the handful of mourners at her funeral, "was sacrificed on the altar of some primitive, pagan and bloodthirsty god whose name has long since been forgotten but whose ugly head has once more raised itself."

The McCullough tragedy, he declared with mounting Old Testament fury, "is proof of the evil which takes possession of people's minds, twists their thinking and goes about in the guise of being God-guided and God-annointed."

Tolton's "pagan god" had come to town that January of 1952 with all the hype and razzmatazz of a snake oil salesman. For weeks, half-page advertisements in the Winnipeg newspapers had been announcing, "A.C. Valdez, Jr. Revival and Healing Campaign. Over one million people have heard him speak. Fifty thousand conversions in fifteen months. God has given him the gift of healing."

There were pictures of the peppy little preacher from Phoenix, Arizona, wearing a natty bow tie and clasping a large Bible. Healing cards, it was announced, would be handed out to the afflicted by Valdez's father, the Reverend A.C. Valdez, Sr., every afternoon prior to the big evening healing service at the 3,000-capacity Winnipeg roller rink.

In their modest one-and-a-half-storey suburban home on Carman Avenue, Gavin and Lillian McCullough awaited Valdez's arrival in town as though it were the second coming. The McCulloughs were familiar figures at King Memorial United Church, which they had attended for fifteen years and where the fifty-one-year-old Gavin, a meek, retiring fellow who was office manager at the Winnipeg Chamber of Commerce, was a steward.

But Mrs. McCullough, a fifty-two-year-old housewife, hungered for a deeper spiritual experience than the comfortable, middle-of-the-road United Church could offer. One night as they talked to Tolton, their minister, she looked up at the stars, her eyes alight. "You know," she said, with awesome certainty, "the Lord will come at any time now."

Seeking that experience, Mrs. McCullough got Gavin and Martha, the cheerful little girl they had adopted at the age of six months, to accompany her to various evangelical churches. Their son Lorne, aged twenty-one, an accountancy student at the University of Manitoba, tried to keep a discreet distance from his parents' new-found fervour.

On the opening night of his healing campaign on January 6, Valdez more than lived up to the expectations of his gullible flock. "You will see miracles before your eyes," he proclaimed, going down on his haunches, then leaping into the air like a jack-in-the-box. "If you are sincere, the sky's the limit," he shouted as people on crutches, in wheel chairs, and those carrying crippled children and sickly babies pressed forward to receive his miraculous touch.

And sure enough, six deaf people claimed they could suddenly hear, and a blind woman said she could see. "Hallelujah!" shouted Lillian McCullough, her face glowing with rapture as she clutched her husband's arm. After that the McCulloughs went to the healing meetings nearly every night.

One evening Tolton and a group of United Church ministers went to see the new competition in town. "There was a woman there from Chicago with a blind baby," Tolton recalled for me. "They put the baby on a sort of operating table, and Valdez ordered all the lights turned off. He shone a flashlight in the baby's eyes and shouted, 'In the name of the Father and of the Son and of the Holy Ghost, I command the devil to go out of you!'"

"Imagine!" said Tolton in wonder, "Saying there was a devil in a little baby like that! Then Valdez cried, 'She sees! She sees!' and the whole crowd yelled, 'Hallelujah!' I wanted to jump up and shout, 'Fraud! Liar!' But I didn't," he said regretfully. "I guess sometimes we don't have the courage to do what we should."

But to the McCulloughs, every "miracle" was proof that the Lord was at hand. They began phoning United Church ministers and even office staff at the Chamber of Commerce urging them, commanding them, to attend the Valdez meetings. When old friends of the McCulloughs, Mr. and Mrs. Harry Rempel, were persuaded to go along to a meeting but claimed afterwards not to have seen any evidence of miracles, they were accused of having the devil in them. And at the end of an incoherent three-hour telephone conversation with Mrs. Rempel one night, Lillian McCullough shouted, "May God strike you dead."

One night at the roller rink as the cripples thronged forward, Mrs. McCullough turned to her husband, a look of ecstasy on her face, and held out her hand. With little Martha between them, they walked hand in hand down the aisle to the front and kneeled, trembling with excitement as Valdez wrung his hands, threw back his head and pleaded with the Lord to do his stuff.

The next morning, with a little prompting from her mother, Martha declared that Jesus had come to her "in a stream of light." Mrs. McCullough told her daughter, "Martha Louise, you won't need your glasses any more." She didn't wear them again, but as Lorne McCullough cynically observed, "She never wore them before very much either."

As the week of healing services came to an end, Mrs. McCullough's religious frenzy mounted. Now she was telling people that since going through the healing line she too had acquired the healing touch and had the ability to cast out devils. And every morning at 2:00, regular as clockwork, God came to her in visions, she said. Using a handkerchief touched by Valdez, she tried to restore the sight of a blind woman but, no doubt inexperienced in working miracles, she did not succeed.

At the last service on Sunday, Valdez claimed to have had a vision. "The windows of heaven opened, and all the blessings of heaven descended on Winnipeg, affecting every home. Winnipeg will be turned upside down—no, right side up," he told the gasping crowd. He added a warning: "My little ones, you will be persecuted."

At 1:00 A.M. on Wednesday, January 24, Lillian McCullough shook her husband awake. She had had another vision and had been told, "The bridegroom cometh immediately." She had been chosen, she told her husband, to announce the second coming that would occur within ten days.

McCullough phoned his office to say he wouldn't be coming to work, and the couple spent their whole time praying and fasting, living only on fruit juice. "You won't need to go to school any more," Mrs. McCullough told Martha, "The Saviour is coming."

When they weren't praying, they were on the phone haranguing friends. One unfortunate United Church min-

ister was awoken at 2:30 A.M. by a call from an almost incoherent Mrs. McCullough calling on him to repent.

Thursday morning Lorne was preparing to leave for his
part-time job when his mother came into the room. "Have
you prayed aloud this morning?" she demanded.

"I prayed last night, Mom. I've got to hurry to get to
work," he replied.

"You will not leave this house until you have confessed
your sins and received the Holy Ghost," his mother said,
and called out to her husband. Gavin, normally a man of
humble demeanor with a weak, down-turning mouth,
seemed transformed by godly wrath when he came into the
bedroom. Inspired by his wife, he forced the sobbing boy to
his knees, ripping his shirt and dislocating the youngster's
shoulder.

It was 11:00 P.M. when Lorne returned home and heard
his parents still praying in their room. He was getting
undressed in his downstairs bedroom when his mother
appeared in her nightdress looking distracted. She asked
again if he'd prayed aloud. This time when his father
arrived Lorne meekly got down on his knees, and soon after
his parents left him in peace. Quietly, purposefully, the boy
began collecting his belongings, and around 1:00 A.M. he
stole away.

In their room the McCulloughs took turns keeping
watch for the coming of the Lord, one praying while the
other slept. They interrupted their spiritual exercises only
to, in McCullough's quaint phrase, "defile the Lord."

In the early morning Mrs. McCullough had another
vision, and Gavin prayed and kept watch as she journeyed
through the world of spirits, moaning and crying out at
intervals. Around 6:00 A.M. they went downstairs looking
eagerly for signs of miracles; they found Lorne's empty
room, his clothes, suitcase and camera gone.

"He has the devil in him for sure," said his mother
angrily. "Come, Gavin, we must pray for him to be saved,"
she said, leading the way back to their bedroom. They were

still praying fervently when the door opened; Martha Louise stood rubbing her eyes and looking in curiously.

That Friday was a typical Winnipeg winter day, the temperature hovering around −20°C, the snow brilliant under a clear blue sky. As she was clearing up after lunch, Mrs. Herbert Dettman glanced out of the window of her Carman Avenue home—then looked again in disbelief.

On a vacant lot beside her home she saw a couple, the man barefoot in his nightshirt, the woman wearing slippers and a housecoat over her nightdress, kneeling and praying at opposite ends of a stack of iron pipes. As Mrs. Dettman watched, the couple got up, came towards each other with a look of ecstasy and embraced. She went to the phone and called the police.

Constable A.P. Ives arrived at the McCulloughs' home minutes later and found them praying. "Is there anyone else in the house?" he asked. "Yes," said Mrs. McCullough, as if it were an irrelevancy, "our daughter is upstairs."

Detective Inspector (later Police Chief) George Blow will never forget the scene he encountered upon arriving at the house shortly afterwards. "It was like entering a religious place," he told me. Religious tracts, many of them put out by Valdez, were scattered around, and from the front room he could hear the sound of the McCulloughs praying aloud. They were on their knees in front of the chesterfield, Gavin meekly repeating prayers after his wife. "Repeat after me," she said. "Repeat after me," parrotted her husband as though he were in a trance.

"If the devil has left you, come over here and kiss me and put your arms around me and hug me," she said. And in front of the astonished policeman, Gavin hugged and kissed his wife as if hypnotized.

"He was completely under her domination," said Blow, retired now and still living in Winnipeg. A few minutes later she told him, "If the devil has left you, prove it by putting all these men out of the house."

Fire came into McCullough's watery eyes behind the

rimless glasses. He drew himself up, pointed to the door and bellowed, "In the name of the Lord, leave this house!" The police tried to calm the wild-eyed couple, explaining they were only there to help. Then Blow went upstairs and pushed open the rear bedroom door.

In his time the inspector had seen more than his share of bloodshed, but this was something new: Martha Louise's little body lay on the bed, the head bloody where it had been smashed, bruises on her throat where she had been strangled. Tufts of her fair hair were scattered on the flannel sheet as though she had been assaulted by a wild animal. "She was just a young and innocent child," he said, shaking his head.

Later a police matron took Mrs. McCullough, still praying and muttering, upstairs and when she left the living room Blow was amazed at the transformation in McCullough. "He calmed right down when she left," he recalled. "He had a dull look on his face, bewildered. He got up, took a cushion from a stool, and told me, 'Sit down and make yourself comfortable. I want to tell you what happened.' "

That morning, he said, Martha had come to their room. "We told her Lorne was away and that the devil had him, and asked her to pray with us. Lillian knew the devil was in Martha Louise too. She tried to shake it out of her, but I interfered. Martha Louise was crying and was under the power of the devil. Lillian threatened to kill her and started banging her head on the floor."

The little suburban living room was dead quiet as the policemen copied down the words of this strange father who seemed almost to be talking in his sleep. "Then Lillian grabbed the bottle and hit her over the head with it several times. She called me because she did not have strength enough. I took the bottle and hit her [Martha] several times as hard as I could, but even then she was still breathing. Then I took my two hands and choked her and kneeled on her chest and finally stopped her breathing. She's safe in the hands of the Lord now," he said casually.

Upstairs, Mrs. McCullough was savagely exultant as,

still kneeling, she told the police, "He [Gavin] looks and acts crazy, but I brought him out of hell. We had to finish her [Martha] off. She was mocking God: she would not get down on her knees and pray."

As they prepared to take McCullough away, the police noted that his eye was swollen. Yes, he admitted, after the killing the devil was in him and his wife had tried to beat it out of him by hitting him with the city directory. "It almost came out—but not quite," he said. So Lillian had suggested he should walk barefoot in the snow to see if that would get the devil out. The next day McCullough had to be carried into court because his feet were frostbitten and bandaged. He still seemed to be in a daze.

Led into the courtroom, Mrs. McCullough smiled fleetingly, not seeming to notice her husband. Then suddenly she seemed to see a vision at the back of the courtroom. Her face went pale. "Gavin! Gavin!" she screamed, then waved at the apparition. As constables tried to restrain her and lead her away, she was still crying her husband's name. In her cell she smashed a light bulb, declaring that she, the chosen of God, could walk on broken glass without coming to harm.

Outrage swept through the prairie city as the details of the prayer-killing emerged. From their pulpits that Sunday, ministers denounced Valdez—by then safely in Toronto on the next leg of his faith healing tour—as a charlatan.

"It is too awful to contemplate," the Reverend W.G. Martin declared from the pulpit of Grace United Church, "that a man whose picture appeared in the advertising columns of our press with a Bible in his hand should hoodwink the people. By extravagantly sensational and childishly crude methods, he worked upon their [the McCulloughs'] emotions to the point that they became mentally unbalanced. The time has come," he said, "to protest against this hocus-pocus of religious humbug and hypocrisy."

At King Memorial that Sunday, as a *Free Press* reporter observed, a ray of sunshine, as if guided by an unseen hand, beamed through a stained glass window on the McCulloughs' empty pew.

At the inquest the coroner, Dr. Athol Gordon, told the jury, "It is entirely appalling that there are these stirrings of the emotions of unstable people by others who come and go and leave the city with a sizeable collection. You will no doubt wonder whether this is religion or not."

During their trials, Gavin and Lillian McCullough were found not guilty of murder by reason of insanity. Dr. Thomas A. Pincock, the provincial psychiatrist, explained that McCullough had been suffering a rare condition called *folie à deux* under which he had, as it were, become "infected" by his wife's insanity. He had been totally under her influence, he said.

Both were detained "at the pleasure of the lieutenant-governor," and after serving only four years of his sentence, Gavin McCullough was released from Headingly Jail and resumed his mouselike existence as an office accountant—taking care to visit his wife at Portage la Prairie women's prison every week.

After fifteen years, Mrs. McCullough too was released, and the McCulloughs bought a little home on Gore Avenue in Winnipeg. Five years ago, said Mrs. McCullough, eighty when I spoke to her, her husband was "promoted to greater glory"—he died in his sleep. She buried him in a pasteboard box beside Martha Louise in Elmwood cemetery; the money saved by paying only $225 for his funeral she donated to the Salvation Army.

"He was the best husband there ever was," she said. Alone afterwards in the Gore Avenue house, she found the gardening and other chores too much for her. "I am not a person to hear voices, but the Lord told me to get out of there," she said. "There's no question about it, the Lord found the apartment for me where I'm living now."

Looking back, she said, "I had the sweetest little daughter—if I had been in my right mind it would never have happened. But," she added, "it was for the glory of God, what happened."

She bore no grudge against Valdez, who died several years ago (although his father, the Reverend A.C. Valdez, Sr., is still living, though bedridden, in Phoenix). And in her last years Lillian McCullough is particularly comforted that the Lord has manifested himself to her yet again.

After a particularly tiring day some time ago, she told me, she lay down on her bed and dozed. "I suddenly awakened, and there was Gavin's face on the pillow right beside me and it was just beautiful. I was spellbound—and if he didn't open his eyes and smile at me!"

Toot, Toot, Tootsie! Goo' Bye

Regina, the capital city of Saskatchewan, presented in the early 1950s the well-scrubbed and orderly appearance of a military base. Neat little white houses lined straight, tree-shaded streets to the edge of the prairie, and the presence in the legislature of a socialist government headed by a former Baptist minister, Tommy Douglas, only seemed to confirm the city's aura of innocence and purity.

But when John Tudor was murdered, there slithered out from the dark underside of the city the most unlikely collection of strange and degenerate characters the respectable citizens of Regina had ever set eyes on.

Bloated and boozy, this motley crew was headed by Tootsie La Fleche (pronounced, naturally, La Flesh), a promiscuous 300-pound woman with the mind of a child. She was, in the words of one policeman who will never forget her, "a barrel of blubber whose price was a bottle of beer."

But confronted with the classic problem of how to dispose of a body—a challenge that has defeated some of the coolest minds in the murder business—Tootsie, in fear and naivety, resorted to a strategem so breathtakingly simple yet unconventional that it nearly succeeded.

John Tudor had started life in Romania as Mihaill Todor, but in 1912 he joined the flood of East European immigrants filling the empty spaces in Canada's West and homesteaded near Wheatstone, in southern Saskatchewan.

By the 1950s we find Todor, who preferred now to be called John or Mike Tudor, seventy-four and well provided for but, with his children grown up and far away in Toronto and Detroit, living a lonely existence in a dilapidated three-room bungalow in the east end of Regina. In its grander days the neighbourhood had been called Tuxedo Park; now the police referred to it derisively as "Bohunk Town," in reference to its many East European residents.

Although Tudor's wooden house was little more than a shack, he also owned a house which occupied four city lots. Because he frequently went away, working for stretches as a construction labourer, he had a law firm collect the rents and pay the bills on the property. After a few drinks Tudor would confide to friends: "I got my money stuffed in my mattress. But don't think nobody can steal it. I got a gun right by my bed and a big stick." He told neighbour Carol Frost that he had $40,000 hidden, and even showed her the gun.

Then, in the fall of 1953, Tudor was foolish enough to let Tootsie La Fleche into his life. Tootsie, thirtyish—she wasn't sure of her age—had spent time in jails and mental hospitals coping with drug and drink problems and had been married four times, first at the age of thirteen. Soon after she moved into the middle room in Tudor's house, ostensibly as housekeeper, she added him to her list of husbands. But, she was to relate, she only stayed with him a week "because he was hard to get along with." So she turned her abundant affections to one John Levitt, a man with whom she had been living common-law, and also provided consolation for Joe Jakubco, aged sixty-five, a Yugoslav who had moved into Tudor's back room as a boarder.

On Christmas Eve, Tudor went to supper with his old friends, Mr. and Mrs. John Yorga, who had known him since homesteading days, and told them to be sure to come over to his place on January 7 to celebrate the Eastern Orthodox Christmas. "I'm going to roast a duck. We'll have a feast," he promised. The next day Mrs. Yorga saw Tudor at St. John's Greek Orthodox Church. After the service Tudor seemed on edge. "I got to get home. There's a wild bunch of men and women in my house. I got to look after the place," he told Mrs. Yorga. She never saw him again.

Tudor had also invited another old crony, Alex Bogdan, over for the January 7 feast and had asked his neighbour, Carol Frost, to keep her Christmas tree and bring it with her to the dinner. But when the guests arrived, Tootsie told them Tudor had gone away to Cupar, north of the city. Suspicious, Bogdan called again a few days later to be told, "Oh, Mike came back, but then he went away again to Kayville." To some, she said he had gone to Windsor, to others, Detroit. She even bandied about a story that he had died in a senior citizens' home in Windsor, and because Tudor's movements had always been unpredictable his friends generally accepted the stories. The world forgot John Tudor.

The law firm of Fraser, Keith and Nicol continued to collect the rent and pay the bills on Tudor's other property; city hydro meter readers continued to read the outside meter, and the bills were always paid. Tootsie continued to live in the middle room containing the wood-burning cookstove, giving frequent parties, doing a little bootlegging on the side and entertaining a succession of disreputable and often inebriated men friends. Carol Frost noticed one difference: every night now Tootsie would come to her house to use the phone to call a cab. "I wonder where she gets the money?" Mrs. Frost wondered.

Soon two more roomers, Ted Walters and Jake Dyck, moved in and, Tootsie explained later with a throaty chuckle, she shared her bed with both of them, pushing the scrawny little Walters out on the floor when she'd had enough of him. There was only one rule in this liberal household: no one, Tootsie insisted, must go into John Tudor's locked front bedroom. "Mike left his money there and told me to keep everybody out," she would say.

Twice Walters saw her unlock the room, but on both occasions she was careful to keep the door shut while inside. Then around July, Walters complained there was a strange smell and a lot of flies around the house. "It's some cabbages rotting in the basement," explained Tootsie. When another friend, Evelyn Burke, complained about the smell, Tootsie said, "Maybe it's a dead cat, or some of old Tudor's dirty wine."

Mrs. Burke went up to the locked door, noticing that the cracks were stuffed with rags. "You should clean it up," she said.

"All right, all right," snapped Tootsie, pushing her away. "I've got the key, I'll get around to it." To another friend, Edith Lavallie, who tried the door, she said, "The old man's got $1,500 in there." He'd left after they'd had a fight, and she had to run and lock herself in the outhouse because he was going after her with a bat, she said.

In August 1954, Tootsie moved in with Mrs. Burke. She seemed depressed and was taking aspirins for her frequent headaches. The roomers left, and a neighbour called police because the house appeared to be unlocked. Regina police checked the house and, not noticing anything amiss, put a padlock on the door; they made a note to check the house regularly in future as an unoccupied abode. The meter reader noticed in September that no electricity had been consumed.

The house stood deserted that winter, the yard full of junk, the snow on the path untrodden. Meanwhile, Mrs. Yorga had checked into the story about Tudor dying in an old people's home in Windsor and found it wasn't true. On April 10, 1955, Pat Ryan, a professional hockey player and longtime friend of the Tudor family, got a letter from Tudor's daughter Mary who lived in Detroit saying she was worred about her father. He used to get a neighbour to write for him, she said, but they hadn't heard from him in over a year. Ryan went down to the McKay Street house and found it sadly dilapidated. The door was padlocked, and he could not see inside because the blinds were drawn. He went to the police the next day.

The smell was the first thing that hit the officers who unlocked the door. "You took a deep breath, then you plunged in," recalled Peter Darke, an identification officer who was one of the first on the scene. When officers broke open the locked front bedroom door, the scene that met them was grotesque. The room was in semi-darkness. Newspapers were pasted on the windows, but they could make out Christmas decorations smothered, like everything else in the room, with a thick layer of dust. Dead flies lay everywhere, and on the maggot-infested bed lay the mummified remains of what fifteen months before had been John Tudor.

"The windows faced west, so in summer it must have gotten pretty hot in there. It really cooked. That's why Tootsie papered over the windows," said Darke, who is now retired. "We found the flowerpot with the paste still in it in her room." A fly spray also testified to her efforts to keep the ghastly process in the front room under control. "At first I thought it was just a case of sudden death," said Darke, but when the coroner turned over the body clad in its underwear, it was apparent that the cheekbone had been broken.

The thick dust made it impossible to detect any fingerprints, and blood spattered all over the ceiling above the bed "powdered into dust if you even breathed on it," recalled Darke. Outside, the yard was full of sticks and pipes, any one of which could have been used as the murder weapon, but the police soon found a hammer bearing traces of blood. "When I got home that night, I burned all my clothes," said Darke emphatically. "I've smelled a lot of things in my time, but that was the worst."

Dr. W.H. Houston, faced with the unpleasant task of performing the autopsy, found that Tudor's skull had been fractured in a number of places, causing death. And then,

as Dr. Houston pried open the clenched fist of the mummified remains, he discovered the solitary clue to the identity
of the assailant: grasped in the palm and sticking from
between the fingers was a hank of grey and black hair—
eighty-one strands in all—pulled from the attacker's head
by the roots in Tudor's dying moments.

Regina police, dealing with their first murder case in sixteen years, immediately arrested Walters and Jakubco and
Cecilia LaSwisse, habitués of the McKay Street house, as
material witnesses, and began a provincewide search for
Tootsie and Jake Dyck. Three days later Tootsie and Jake
drove down from Liberty, Saskatchewan, and turned themselves in.

"I didn't kill the old man," insisted Tootsie.

"Who did, then?" an officer asked.

"It was Nick Hordenchuk," she said without hesitation.
The police net quickly brought in Hordenchuk, a reformed
drunk who had made several visits to the McKay Street
house, and he was charged with murder. "I lived with old
Tudor one winter. He was a great old guy," said Hordenchuk when I found him in the tiny apartment where he
now lives in downtown Regina. "And the cops knew almost
from the beginning I didn't kill him. They checked up on
me, see, and they found I was down the other end of the
city drinking a gallon of wine that New Year's Day when he
was killed.

"Tootsie fingered me. I'd never seen her but two or three
times. Mine was the first name that came into her head,"
said Hordenchuk, whose squashed nose and ravaged face
still betray his drinking years. And he paid a terrible price
for her accusation.

"When the police released me, little kids on the street
yelled, 'You murderer.' Guys would call me 'a murderin'
s.c.b.' I hadn't taken a drink in eight months. I was on a
program. But that made me so mad I went back on the
booze, and I didn't stop drinking again 'til 1969. I lost fourteen years out of my life through that case," he said bit-
terly.

The police knew from the laboratory tests that the hair in Tudor's hand belonged almost certainly to Jake Dyck, a hefty farm labourer with an artificial leg and cold blue eyes; Dyck was charged with murder, and Tootsie was charged as an accessory.

From the start, the case was bedevilled. On the first day of the trial, a member of the jury was stricken with three heart attacks, and the trial proceeded with eleven jurors who, after deliberating for ten hours, could not agree on their verdict. A second trial also ended with a hung jury, and it was not until after a third trial in April 1956 that Dyck was finally convicted of the murder and sentenced to death. Throughout these lengthy proceedings, Tootsie La Fleche and her strange world of underground characters never failed to fascinate the crowds that filled the courtroom.

"They were like characters out of a Hogarth painting. Dickens would have had a field day with them," said G.H.M. Armstrong, who early in the proceedings acted as Tootsie's lawyer. "Tootsie was completely without any concern about right or wrong. I would go and see her in jail to get instructions, and she would spend the whole time telling me stories about the other prisoners. She didn't seem to care a damn what happened to her."

In the witness box, Tootsie, her calculating eyes almost lost in the rolls of her doughy face, fascinated the lawyers as, interrupting herself with a high, nutty laugh, she related the details of her bizarre sex life at McKay Street.

Turning to the murder, she said that after supper on New Year's Eve 1953, "John and I were playing cards for a while and drinking wine. He got sleepy and went to bed." She went out because, as she explained, "I like to take long walks when I'm drunk." She met Jake Dyck, they returned home and she knocked on Tudor's window to get him to let them in. The three of them drank homemade wine laced with sugar for extra zip, "and I got plastered," she said. Then, she claimed, Tudor and Dyck had a disagreement over some money that Dyck said Tudor owed him for some painting he'd done. Dyck and Tudor went in the other room, and she heard the old man cry out, "Why, why, why?"

"I went in there. John was on the bed, lying on his side. There was blood all over the floor and running from his head. I stepped in it."

Did Dyck have anything in his hand? Crown prosecutor R.M. Barr asked. Without a word Tootsie raised her hand and pointed dramatically at the exhibit table.

"What are you pointing at?" Barr asked.

"That hammer," she said, indicating the hammer which had been entered as an exhibit.

Dyck, she said, "turned around on me and said if I opened my mouth I would get the same thing." She kept $210 she found in Tudor's wallet, and Dyck kept $1,500 he had discovered in Tudor's money belt. After Dyck left, "I was afraid to move away or call the police. I thought the first thing they would do is lock me up and accuse me of this thing." Months later, when they were both working on a farm, she had seen Dyck bury the $1,500 in two tin cans, she testified.

But at the second trial, Tootsie's evidence contradicted her statements at the preliminary hearing and first trial on a number of points. Mr. Justice Stewart McKercher held up his hand: "Now, Miss La Fleche, you swore to tell the truth."

A sly expression found its way across the vast reaches of Tootsie's face. "Oh no, I didn't, judge. You didn't hear me right," she said. "I said in a whisper, 'I swear to tell anything *but* the truth.' " Everyone in that crowded courtroom roared with laughter. She was incorrigible, and one of the several judges she appeared before was to call her "an admitted unmitigated liar."

"She was a dangerous woman," recalled Judge Lloyd Hipperson, who defended Dyck during his numerous trials and who for years afterwards had to tolerate legal colleagues humming "Toot, Toot, Tootsie! Goo' Bye," when they passed him in the hall. "I asked her one day why she had accused Nick Hordenchuk of the murder. She looked at me with such venom, and when she spoke she just spat the words out. 'To save his neck,' she said, jerking her thumb at Jake."

Dyck denied his guilt, and said he was at a friend's house that night. Given the fact he could only walk slowly with his artificial leg, he claimed he couldn't possibly have walked the several kilometres from his home to McKay Street and committed the murder at the time Tootsie said he had. But the evidence of the hair sample, attested to by a Royal Canadian Mounted Police lab expert, seemed irrefutable.

"I had searched high and low to see if I could find anything relating to the probabilities of two people having the same sort of hair," said defence counsel Hipperson. He resisted the temptation to ask the RCMP corporal the question in the event that the answer might be damaging to Dyck, but in the corridor after the corporal's testimony at the third trial his curiosity got the better of him. "Are the chances a million to one against it?" he asked the officer. "Oh, my goodness, no," he replied. It was not at all uncommon for two people to have almost identical hair. Hair was not like fingerprints, said the policeman.

Hipperson went back into the courtroom cursing his bad luck for not having asked the question in court. But just then the foreman of the jury asked if the RCMP officer could be recalled to the stand. "Corporal, what would the probabilities be of two people having the same kind of hair?" the foreman asked.

"That corporal looked down at me. He was so annoyed. He was sure I'd fixed it somehow," said Hipperson, laughing. With Tootsie discredited and the hair sample now very much in question, the way was opened for an appeal court to overturn Dyck's conviction and death sentence.

Hipperson had lived the case with Dyck for more than a year, visiting him in death row at Prince Albert Jail—and knew almost as little about his client at the end as he did at the beginning. "He was the most unshakeable person I ever met. He never showed any emotion, even in the death cell. He was a very calculating man with those blue eyes that looked right through you," recalled the judge. "I never asked him if he did the dastardly job. I didn't want to know." On the day Dyck was released after his successful appeal, "he didn't have a nickel, so I took him home to my place for lunch. I even got him a job on a road construction gang and drove him out to it. He never so much as said thank you."

Who murdered John Tudor? To this day Crown prosecutor Barr believes it was not Tootsie, and cites a letter written to her mother (and intercepted) in which she wrote, "I'll hang for it, but I didn't do it." But it's difficult to believe that Tootsie didn't have her eye on the old man's money all along, that she didn't meet Jake by prearrangement New Year's Eve to bring him back to Tudor's house. Whether, hefty as she was, she helped hold down the powerful old man while Jake, one-legged and easily thrown off balance, bludgeoned him, there's no way of knowing. Whatever her involvement, Tootsie in the end got by far the worst of the deal.

Under the rolls of flesh there must have been something capable of fear and remorse; during one of the trials she swallowed a bottle of sleeping pills in an unsuccessful attempt to commit suicide. As soon as Dyck was convicted and sentenced to death, she was tried and sentenced to five years in Kingston women's penitentiary as an accessory. When Dyck's conviction was quashed she too could have appealed, but no one thought to tell her and she did her time. Within a few days of her release from jail in 1960, she was found dead beside an Ontario highway after having been run over. Vengeance? Suicide? Drunkeness? We'll never know.

I prefer to think of her as she left the courtroom that last day when she'd been given the five-year sentence. "She didn't look so bad then," recalled prosecutor Barr. "She'd lost a lot of weight during all those months in prison. She was down to about 220 pounds. I was hurrying out of the back door of the courtroom when she spotted me in the corridor. I was just squeezing past when she grabbed me around the neck and kissed me.

"'Thanks, Mr. Barr,' she said, and I think she really meant it."

The Professor Panicked

Primulas were blooming in the gardens of the Empress
Hotel in Victoria, the eternal springtime capital of British
Columbia. Elderly ladies, wattles a-tremble, were sipping
their afternoon tea as Keith Latta, a chunky man with the
rapid movements of a Rod Steiger, made his way across the
lobby towards me. We shook hands a trifle nervously and I
suggested, "Let's go up to my room to talk." The genteel tea
hour in this most British of Canadian settings didn't seem
quite the appropriate spot to interview a man serving a life
sentence for murder.

In 1971 Latta, then forty-three, a law professor at
Queen's University in Kingston, Ontario, was happily married with five children and enjoying a growing reputation
for his pioneering work in computerizing the legal system.
When I met him early in 1981, he was an inmate of the
William Head penitentiary on Vancouver Island, albeit out
on day parole living in a halfway house in Victoria, and was
about to apply for full parole after completing a term of ten
years in jail for the murder of his former business partner,
Robert Neville.

The murder of Bob Neville, a slick young businessman
and politician with a permanent-press smile, on a quiet
summer Sunday morning in Edmonton, Alberta, is a classic whodunit, which, I would submit, has not been solved
to this day. But Latta's conviction for the killing is much
more: it is a revelation of the unpredictability of human
behaviour, and whether or not you believe Keith Latta
guilty, the case is a profound indictment of our legal system.

Upstairs in my large, high-ceilinged room we ordered
coffee; Latta lit a thin cigar and explained why, even with
the prospect of freedom ahead, he was still fighting his conviction. "People think because I may get out of jail soon
that what happend in the past is just academic," he said.
"Yet I am stuck the rest of my life a convicted murderer. I
have been ruined financially, I have been disbarred and
have lost my profession. I don't intend to let this thing die
as long as I am alive."

That fateful Sunday a decade ago, Latta rose late in his
room at the Edmonton Inn where he had been staying on a
brief visit from his home in Kingston, Ontario. He thought
of the pleasant time he'd spent the day before with his
mother and young sister Shirley at Elk Island Park, east of
the city, where, walking along the beach, he told them:
"I'm the happiest I've ever been in my life. It's too bad I
didn't realize sooner how much I enjoy teaching."

Latta had grown up in Edmonton, graduating from the
University of Alberta law school in 1955. In 1968 he had
gone east to Queen's University in Kingston as a full professor, largely to pursue research work on his system for
computerizing law precedents.

After breakfast that Sunday, Latta returned to his room
and dialed Bob Neville's number at Neville World Travel
Services Ltd. on Jasper Avenue. Keith Latta and Bob
Neville had been partners in the business until a short time
before. Neville had bought him out, and Latta's appointment that morning was to discuss the settlement of the life
insurance which, as in any partnership, they had held on

each other's lives. Neville had also intimated that he wanted to discuss blackmail threats that had been made against him because of his extramarital affairs with two women, one of whom had supposedly become pregnant. The number, when Latta dialed, was busy.

Meanwhile Neville, a thirty-six-year-old Edmonton school trustee who had recently made an unsuccessful bid for a Progressive Conservative party nomination, had left home early, calling at the Chateau Lacombe Hotel for his usual Sunday steak and egg breakfast.

He stopped at the smoke shop in the Corona Hotel to buy cigars, then headed next door to his office where, just before 11:00 A.M., he put in a call to his wife who was holidaying in Honolulu and from whom he was in the process of getting divorced. Then, as Neville got down to his weekend work, phoning clients about airline reservations, the unlocked door to the travel agency opened.

* * *

Two hours later a woman walking along Jasper Avenue happened to glance into the travel agency window. She ran to a taxi parked across the lane. "There's a man lying on the floor in there. You better call the police," she said.

Constable Paul Cetinski peered through the window, then walked into the travel agency. Bob Neville lay face down in the front office in a pool of blood, two bullet holes in his back. There was, it turned out, no dearth of clues for the Edmonton police to work with.

Neville had been shot twice in the back; another shot had been fired from the front with a .32 revolver at close quarters. Two of the bullets were found in the body, the third on the floor of Neville's office. On the floor police found a roll of paper secured with an elastic and containing a bus terminal locker key. The paper appeared to be a hand-drawn map of downtown Edmonton which indicated the travel agency; notations were written in Italian. At the rear of the agency, police found a photocopying machine, still on, insurance documents and an envelope bearing

Latta's name and address and a dead cigar from which only two or three puffs had been taken.

With the key, police opened locker 55 at the Union Bus Depot and found a parcel wrapped in a July 9 copy of the Calgary *Herald*. It contained a brown leather glasses case, an English–Italian dictionary, a Michelin map of Italy, a zippered black leather case, twenty-two live rounds of .32 calibre ammunition, eighteen spent .32 cartridges and two newspaper photographs of Bob Neville.

Keith Latta, meanwhile, had checked out of the Edmonton Inn at 12:04 P.M., turned in his rental car at Edmonton International Airport at 1:30, and caught a 3:00 P.M. flight for Toronto. On arriving home in Kingston, he found a phone message from an Edmonton friend who informed him of Neville's death. It was 4:35 A.M. Kingston time. Latta put through a call to the Edmonton police.

He told Detective Norman Koch of his visit to Edmonton and explained what he knew of threats against Neville's life because of the travel agent's philandering. He was supposed to meet Neville Sunday morning, but when he didn't get a call from him he'd checked out of his hotel and returned to Toronto, Latta said. In a later phone conversation with Inspector Alfred LeFeuvre, Latta mentioned that he met Neville earlier in his visit to Edmonton, "so I expect you will find some of my fingerprints around." Would he, the inspector asked, send along a set of palm and fingerprints through the Ontario Provincial Police, "just for elimination purposes?"

"Certainly," said Latta.

The prints were decisive: they corresponded exactly to palm prints and fingerprints on the map and the newspaper found in the locker. Edmonton police felt they had their motive in the insurance papers found on the photocopier. The documents showed Latta held a double indemnity policy on Neville's life for $75,000.

On Saturday, six days after the killing, Latta pulled into his driveway after going grocery shopping for his wife. A large car swooped in behind him, the doors sprang open and the burly forms of Detective Robert Joyce and Staff Sergeant Joe Poss emerged.

"They asked me if I was Keith Latta. I could tell by their nervousness that they were there to arrest me," said Latta. When they warned him about making a statement, he answered, "Lookit, I'm a lawyer and a law professor, you don't have to tell me about the law." That's how naive he was.

He was not allowed to go into the house to explain to his wife Bernadene ("Dene"), and as he left she thought he was going downtown for questioning. At Kingston police headquarters he met Inspector LeFeuvre who told him: "We know you didn't pull the trigger, but if you are involved you are as guilty as if you had."

"I didn't do it," Latta told them. But the officers asked for no statement. Their job now was to prove his involvement.

In the weeks that followed, Latta considered hiring Arthur Maloney, the crack criminal lawyer from Toronto, to defend him, but was advised not to because it would arch the backs of the Alberta legal establishment. Instead he hired Cameron Steer, an establishment lawyer whose experience was mainly in civil rather than criminal cases. In a long list of mistakes made by Latta, the supposed law expert, this was to be crucial.

The six-day trial began on December 13, 1971, in Edmonton's old courthouse, in weather that often hit −30°C. Reading the evidence today it's difficult to believe that a man's freedom could depend on such a gossamer of confusing irrelevancies and disconnected pieces of information. And although the one hard fact that stood out was Latta's fingerprints on the items in the locker, defence counsel Steer foolishly tried to attack the credibility of the fingerprint expert.

No prints had been found in the travel agency; no one had seen Latta there, so the Crown had no way of placing him at the scene of the murder. A gun found in a pond in an Edmonton park after the murder was entered as an exhibit, and a Royal Canadian Mounted Police ballistics expert claimed there was "a weak probability" it was the murder weapon.

Two women with whom Neville had had affairs testified that they knew of no blackmail threats and that neither had become pregnant. A Kingston insurance agent, Harry Kingstone, gave confusing and, as it turned out, misinformed evidence about the insurance policies Latta and Neville held on each others lives. Witnesses were called to trace Neville and Latta's movements on the day of the murder.

And that was that. The confused jury must have been waiting to hear Keith Latta's explanation of this curious array of facts, but a behind-the-scenes battle was going on in the defence corner. The evening of the trial's second day, defence counsel Steer told Mrs. Latta that he had changed his mind and would not put Keith on the witness stand.

In any murder trial, deciding whether to put the accused on the stand is one of the toughest decisions for the defence attorney. If the attorney feels the Crown's case is weak and the client would only make damaging admissions or look bad in the box, the rule of thumb is to keep the accused silent at all costs. There is a risk in not testifying— the jury can think the accused has something to conceal. Steer argued that William Stainton, the fierce Crown prosecutor in the case, would "crucify Keith" (who had not been getting proper sleep at RCMP barracks and was tired). But Latta's wife Dene replied that without her husband's evidence the jury would have no idea of what actually had occurred. When Steer told him the next morning of his decision, Latta, feeling that he was too confused and emotionally involved to properly judge the situation, bowed to Steer's advice.

If the defence calls no witnesses, it has the right to deliver the final summation to the jury—often a decisive advantage. Steer lost out two ways: he called four completely unimportant witnesses to attest to minor details, achieved nothing, and made a fatal blunder in giving the terrier Stainton the last word.

Steer, fatigued by Friday, December 17, when he rose to address the jury, gave a rambling and ineffectual discourse in a voice so quiet the court reporter several times had to ask him to speak up. A tall and distinguished Stainton rose the next morning to deliver a devastating assault. Until Stainton started speaking, Latta told me, he believed the most he would be accused of was co-conspiracy. At the opening of the trial, Stainton had spoken of Latta as having "a serious connection" with the murder. Instead, Stainton, at the climax of his aggressive summation, spoke of "the killer," then, turning slowly and dramatically, pointed at Latta, saying, "who I submit is the accused."

"Cam Steer almost fell off his seat," said Latta. The six hours the jury was out "were the worst of my life," he continued. When I heard the verdict, "Guilty," it "was as if I had been hit over the head with a sledge hammer."

Dene had bought a ticket home to Kingston for her husband, anticipating that he would be found not guilty. Instead she found herself with the dread task of phoning the children with the bad news.

"But Daddy hasn't done anything," she told them.

"Oh, we know that," they replied.

Latta entered Fort Saskatchewan to begin a life sentence with no possibility of parole in less than ten years, but Dene told Keith's family, who had supported him all the way, "I'm not going to take this lying down." Years of futile appeals followed, but it didn't matter what new evidence the Lattas, even resorting to a private detective, dug up, the courts always ruled it inadmissable.

In 1972 an Edmonton cab company supervisor revealed that a Brazilian working as a cabbie in Edmonton, Louis Goncalves, had admitted to him the day after the murder that he had been paid to kill Neville. Located in Brazil by a reporter from the *Edmonton Journal,* Goncalves denied the accusation, but before police could interview him he had disappeared.

A young women who, by remarkable coincidence had since married the foreman of the jury in the Latta trial, testified in court that she had spent two weeks with Neville in

Las Vegas, that he had run up $30,000 in debts and had been threatened with death if he did not pay up at least half the money. Her evidence was discounted as hearsay.

Up to that point no one, apart from Cameron Steer and Dene Latta, had heard Latta's account of what happened the morning of the murder. Finally, in February 1973, Latta gave police the statement they should have had from the start and which the jury should have heard.

Assuming that, when the phone was busy that Sunday, Bob Neville was at his office, and expecting to see other employees there who usually worked a few hours on Sunday, Keith Latta said he parked his rented car behind the Jasper Avenue building. As he passed in front of the window, he saw Neville on the phone in his private office.

The bolt on the front door of the building was thrown so the door would not close, and Latta entered, finding the agency doors also unlocked. Neville signalled for him to sit down while he finished talking to someone on the phone about airline reservations.

He and Neville chatted for a few minutes, then Latta went down the hallway to a poorly lit area near noisy air conditioners at the back of the offices to photocopy the insurance documents for Neville. He switched on the machine and, while he waited for it to warm up, lit a cigar Neville had given him. As he put the first documents on the machine, he became aware of voices in the front office.

"Then I heard a thump against the wall of Bob's private office followed by a terrific explosion." He turned to see two dim figures, haloed against the bright light, running down the hallway towards him. A second shot was fired, the two men struggled backwards; there was a third explosion, and then silence.

"I ran forward and found Bob lying in the middle of the front office. There was no sign of his assailant. I checked Bob's pulse, and there was no sign of life. My immediate reaction was to phone the police. At that moment," he said,

"I noticed there was a piece of paper rolled up in an elastic band on the floor.

"I picked it up. There was one of those coin locker keys inside and a map drawn on a piece of foolscap. What puzzled me was that the words were in a foreign language. My first thought was that this must have been dropped accidentally by the assailant." His heart pounding, in a state of panic, he hurried out of the back door and drove to the bus terminal with some idea, he claims, of finding from the contents of the locker the identity of the killer.

No one was at the lockers. But what would he do if the killer arrived? Latta stood back apprehensively, his eyes glued to locker 55. No one came, so he hurried forward, fumbled the key into the lock and opened it. He found the parcel, sat down on a bench and opened it, leaving the palm and fingerprints that were to convict him, then wrapped it up again, put it back in the locker and returned to the murder scene.

With the body in full view from the street, he'd expected to find the agency swarming with police by now, but it was just as he'd left it. "The only thing that kept going through my mind was how upsetting it would be for my family and for my position back in Kingston to be involved as a witness in such a bizarre matter. I had the overwhelming feeling that I should get the hell out of there."

Hurrying out the back way, he forgot about the documents on the photocopying machine. But as he put his hand in his pocket for the car keys, he felt the map and locker key. "I threw them into the hall," he said, "and left."

It was only on the plane back to Toronto that he fully realized the mess he'd entangled himself in, he said, puffing on his cigar in the hotel room.

Does he say that, in spite of the evidence that convinced a jury, he was not involved in Neville's murder? Keith Latta leaned forward. "I was not implicated, Frank, in any way," he said softly.

Then why had he run out and then lied to the police on the phone? "I felt that just being there would get me into a lot of trouble . . . being suspected," he said. The room was silent as I shuffled through my documents on the case.

"It mentions here that you were brought up in the evangelical faith. Which one?" I asked.

"Oh, you wouldn't have heard of it," he said brushing my question aside. "Plymouth Brethren."

A little understanding dawned. Like Latta, I had grown up in a Brethren home, and perhaps only one brought up in that oppressive atmosphere of rigid Sabbath observance, of constant examination of the conscience for sin, could understand the burden of guilt some former Brethren adherents carry for their lives. In that light it was possible to see Latta, who had preached in gospel halls as a youngster, paralyzed with the fear of exposure as he confronted the body of his dead partner. You will have to make up your own mind about that because no court, it seems, is willing to take up his case again.

In 1976, in an attempt to get his story on the record, Latta took civil action against the London Life Insurance Company to try to force it to pay the $75,000 life insurance on Neville's life. If he thought it would lead the way to a new trial, he was disappointed. Little new evidence was admitted into court. Latta was on the stand for two and a half days, and Virginia Byfield of the magazine *Alberta Report* told me, "He was quiet and convincing."

Mr. Justice W.K. Moore, without further explanation, said he didn't believe Latta, and Latta lost the civil action. Losing was almost inevitable: three weeks before the trial, the Alberta Evidence Act was amended to provide for the admission of the previous criminal conviction to prove guilt in a civil trial. It was referred to in the courtroom as "the Latta amendment."

During the long, dragged-out battle to vindicate Keith Latta, Dene, to preserve her sanity, went to law school at Queen's. In 1977 she graduated, no doubt the first lawyer to get her diploma with a husband serving a life term. Latta was granted a release for the occasion. Through the years Dene Latta has also coped with constant medical crises; two sons have severe kidney disorders.

"When I look at the youngsters, I marvel at how well they have done, but it would be false to suggest we were not affected in many deep ways," she said.

Members of Latta's family, in fact, have poured their lives and money into the fight, organizing themselves so that Keith gets at least one visit from the family every three weeks.

And it goes on. "Our only hope now," said Dene, "is to come up with the real culprit."

"It's the old problem," said Henry Rees, a seventy-eight-year-old Saskatoon lawyer I contacted, who, while never having met Latta, has made a study of his case and has demanded a new trial for him. "It's the little guy against the state, and the state has millions of dollars to carry out the investigation and the little guy has next to nothing. The state doesn't want to open up this case because it reveals a lot of the flaws in the system. The prosecution against Latta was a most vicious sort of thing," said Rees, who has handled murder cases himself. "And it would have made all the difference if he'd been allowed to testify at the original trial. I get the impression that the Alberta lawyers don't want to do anything about it because they don't want to stir up the judges. It's a damned sad thing."

Would the jury, presented with Latta's side of the story, have found him guilty? Crown prosecutor Stainton argued in court that if Neville had been killed by a hit man, that hit man was a remarkably inept killer who had left the oddest sort of evidence behind for no apparent reason.

"But it was known I had an appointment with Bob," said Latta, walking through the hotel gardens as dusk settled on Victoria harbour. "Who would be foolish enough to make an appointment with someone they were going to kill?"

But the insurance? . . . "That would have meant I was planning to murder him since 1965 when we took out the policies," he said.

We stood leaning on the sea wall, the sound of a ship's horn sounding in the distance. "It's been a ten-year nightmare for us," he said. "We only survived because you only get led down into the valley of the shadow of death one step at a time. You always feel that the next step will be the end of the nightmare—but it isn't. It just goes on and on, like a meat grinder. Even if a new trial were granted now, I don't think it would be possible to have one. A lot of the people involved have died. My only hope is that someday I will be given a pardon.

"You know," he said, as we parted, "people think that because they are innocent nothing can happen to them. Well, that's nonsense."

I watched him walk away, a hunched figure striding quickly along the dock, oblivious to the boats and the freewheeling gulls. Even though Keith Latta would soon be freed from prison, he would never be free of that sequence of events that started one quiet Sunday morning on Jasper Avenue.

Who Shot the Scottish Nightingale?

"Say bye-bye to Mommy. Say bye-bye to Daddy." Baby Rosemary, just under a year old, crinkled her pretty blue eyes inside her sunbonnet as the nursemaid, Janet, held her up on the verandah to see her parents off.

"Bye, darling," called Frederick ("Leffy") Lefevre Baker as he backed the car onto Osler Street. "Isn't Janet a treasure!" he remarked to his young wife Doreen ("Queenie"), sitting in the passenger seat. As the car bowled past the lush lawns and rose gardens of fashionable Shaughnessy Heights, it wasn't yet 9:00 A.M., and the heat already shimmered off the road; Saturday, July 26, was to be, in fact, the hottest day of 1924 in Vancouver.

"She certainly loves the baby, but I don't know how long she'll stay," said Queenie, whose sultry, drawling voice had been one of the many things that had attracted Baker when he had married her two years before. "With so many young men after Janet, I'm sure she'll soon find a husband. Sometimes I worry that she isn't careful enough about the young men she takes up with."

It was a glorious time in the golden twenties for the glamourous couple. Within months of their marriage, Leffy, a dashing World War 1 flyer in his late thirties, had taken his bride to Europe for an extended stay in connection with his job as partner in the Baker–Golwynne Chemical Co., a pharmaceutical importing firm. And it was while they were residents in London that they had hired twenty-two-year-old Janet Smith, whose broad accent revealed her Glasgow origins. Looking after the baby brought Janet a mere $20 a month, but she hadn't minded because it gave her a chance first to live in Paris with her employers and then to travel with them to Vancouver.

Back now in their home town, Leffy and Queenie had quickly got back into the social swing; only a day earlier, Baker and his tennis partner had got to the semi-finals of the men's doubles in the Lower Mainland Tennis Championships before gradually succumbing to their opponents and the wilting heat.

Baker stopped the car at an imposing house on Nelson Street. "I'll pick you up later, darling," he said as Queenie got out. "Don't work too hard. It's going to be a scorcher." The old Baker family home on Nelson Street was being readied for Leffy and Queenie to move in; for the meantime, his brother and sister-in-law had let the couple use their Osler Street home while they were away in Europe. As Queenie attended to a few chores before going shopping, Baker headed downtown to make a few business calls before going to his office.

The Osler Street house was a generously proportioned cedar-shingled home set amongst fruit trees where Janet, after her employers left, snuggled the baby and put her down to sleep in the nursery. "I'll have my breakfast now, Wong," she called. Wong Foon Sing came bustling in. "You like egg?" he asked. Kindly, always smiling Wong had worked as a houseboy for the Baker tribe for the past five or six years. After making Janet's breakfast, he began his regular Saturday morning routine—watering and tending the house plants, polishing the brass and shining the hallway floor. As the morning went on the heat became more and more oppressive; his face running with sweat, Wong broke off and went down to his room in the cool basement for a few minutes and smoked a cigarette.

Janet, slender and sturdy in her blue denim smock, white stockings and running shoes, washed out some baby clothes, then, singing a Scottish song at the top of her voice, went outside to hang them up.

"Now will you listen to her," said one of the carpenters, stopping the work he was doing on the house next door. "Isn't she a lovely Scottish nightingale!"

"You can say that again," said his mate, and they sat for a few minutes enjoying the singing until Janet, pretending not to hear their compliments, went downstairs to the basement to iron.

Wong looked at the time. It was nearly lunchtime, and he hurried to the kitchen to peel the potatoes. A few minutes later Wong heard a sharp explosion. He looked out of the kitchen window, thinking perhaps a tire had burst. Then he went to the basement stairs. "Janet!" he called. "Janet!"

Baker was in his office when the phone rang a few minutes after noon. "It's Wong, Mr. Baker. Come quick. Bad trouble." In the incoherent explanation that followed, Baker could only pick out a word he thought was "nursery."

"Oh, my God!" said Baker, banging down the phone and dashing for his car. "The baby!"

Wong was standing in the driveway wringing his hands, his white work apron rolled up, when Baker jumped from his car. "Not baby—nursey. Come quick," said Wong, and they ran down the basement stairs. In the laundry room Janet was lying on her back with her head partly under the laundry tubs. A heavy, long-barrelled .45 army automatic pistol lay on the floor beside her right hand. The still-warm electric iron, its plug pulled from the overhead socket, lay flat on the floor between her right arm and her body. Her eyes were open and staring, and there was a gaping bullet wound above her right eye, a trickle of blood running down her face. A bloodstained towel hung from the wringer and Janet's glasses, broken and blood-spattered, lay on the floor beside her.

Baker, realizing she was beyond help, ran upstairs and phoned the Point Grey municipal police. As he turned from the phone, Wong's apron unfurled; the bottom was covered with blood.

"What happened?" Baker asked.

"Oh, no, Mr. Baker," said Wong, looking down at the apron. "I just get blood on when I bend over nursey." At 12:40 the municipal health officer, Dr. Bertie Blackwood, drove up with Constable James Green. The body was still warm, and Dr. Blackwood estimated death had occurred in the last hour. He noted that Janet's fair hair was matted with blood at the back where the bullet had probably emerged, and he estimated there was about a pint of blood on the floor.

Constable Green, somewhat of an Inspector Clouseau, casually leaned over the body and picked up the gun. "Funny," he said, yanking at the clip and obliterating any fingerprints, "It won't come out."

"Here, man, I'll show you," said the doctor taking hold of the gun and showing the officer how it worked. Green noticed that there were live bullets in the clip and one in the breech, but it didn't enter his head to sniff the barrel to see if the gun had been fired. He picked up a spent cartridge from the floor, not thinking to look around for the slug that had killed Janet. "I thought it was still in her head," he said later.

The gun, Baker told the constable, belonged to his brother; it had been issued to him while he was in the Royal Air Force during the war. The gun had hung in a knapsack in the basement until a few weeks before when Wong, thinking it was dangerous to have it there, had taken it to the attic, where it was hung for safety.

"Well, gentlemen," said Green, drawing himself up with policemanly dignity after one of the shortest, most incompetent murder investigations in his city's history. "It's a clear case of suicide. Clearest case I ever saw." Green went upstairs and phoned the coroner to report. "Is there a doctor present?" the coroner asked. "Yes," said Green. "Then you can have the body removed." At 2:00 P.M. a long black hearse drew up in the driveway, and Janet's remains were slid into the back on a stretcher. Shortly afterwards, her body was being embalmed—and the wounds erased with plaster of paris—at the premises of T. Edwards, undertaker.

Two days later a perfunctory inquest decided that Janet had come to her death accidentally—a polite euphemism for suicide. But they were wrong: Janet Smith had been murdered, and in the next eighteen months the repercussions were to rock Vancouver society and lead to one of the most disgraceful episodes in the history of Canadian law enforcement.

Constable Green hadn't given another thought to the affair for the rest of the weekend; on Monday, returning to the Osler Street house to complete his investigation, he found a bullet lying intact on the basement floor and what seemed to be a bullet mark on the basement wall about two metres from the floor. "Hm . . . interesting," the constable mused, his composure undisturbed.

The apparent suicide of a young woman who only a short time before her death was singing merrily had not gone unnoticed. A brief report on the back page of the *Province* ended, "Her friends speak highly of her, and cannot find any motive for self-destruction."

Rumours began to fly and, at a time when anti-Chinese feelings were strong in British Columbia, suspicion focused on Wong, the twenty-six-year-old houseboy who was the only adult known to have been in the house at the time of the death. The coroner, Dr. W.D. Brydone-Jack, finally spurred into action, visited the undertaker to view the body, and ordered it removed to the morgue for a belated autopsy. A reporter, meanwhile, had phoned provincial Attorney-General Alex Manson to tip him off that there was more to the Janet Smith death than a mere suicide, and Inspector Forbes Cruickshank of the British Columbia Provincial Police was ordered to the case.

Cruickshank's first stop was the morgue, where Dr. A.W. Hunter had just completed the autopsy. "Scandalous!" fumed the doctor as he washed his hands. "It's well-nigh impossible to find out anything when the body's been embalmed. It should never have been allowed. But I'll tell you one thing, inspector," he said. "That little girl could no more have shot herself than she could have jumped over the moon. Now take that thundering great gun she was supposed to have used. I've measured, and the furthest away she could have held it from her is ten and one-half inches, and at that she would have had to hold the damn thing upside down and her skin would have been peppered with powder marks. But look," he said, pulling the sheet from the dead girl's face. "No marks, and not even the undertaker could have gotten those off—they would have been just like tattoos."

Cruickshank nodded. "And look here, inspector," said the doctor, warming to his own argument. "See these burn marks in her armpit? Well there's no burns on the girl's clothing. Very strange! And the burns certainly happened after her death because there's no blistering. And you can't tell me the girl shot herself in the forehead. People killing themselves invariably shoot themselves in the mouth or the ear or the side of the head. And something else," called Hunter as Cruickshank was walking to the door. "I'm not pretending to do your job, but tell me how the girl could have ended up with her head under the laundry tub if she'd just fallen to the ground."

Cruickshank had a lot on his mind as he left. "The iron, now that's very strange," he thought to himself. That afternoon the Baker basement resounded with a series of thuds and clatters as Cruickshank repeatedly shoved the iron off the edge of the ironing board. Every time he did the cord, suspended from an arm on the ceiling to make ironing easier, pulled out of the socket on the iron, rather than out of the overhead socket.

When a second inquest opened on September 4, 1924, such a huge crowd flocked to the Vancouver courthouse that C.W. Craig, the counsel retained by the province, had to climb on someone's shoulders and shout through the transom over the door to be let in. The city's Scottish Societies, eager to protect the interests of the Glasgow lassie, had appointed Alex Henderson as their lawyer and even Wong Foon Sing, no doubt advised by his Tong or Chinese brotherhood, had retained a lawyer. But the most searching questions were asked by James Wilson, foreman of the jury and an ex-Liverpool policeman.

How, he wanted to know, could both the gun and the iron have fallen together? "You either iron or you handle a gun. You don't do both." Why, he asked the red-faced Constable Green, who had been temporarily suspended for incompetence, did he not find the bullet until two days after the death? "I didn't look," said Green lamely.

In a grisly little sideshow, the investigators had secured a corpse from a provincial mental institution and fired .45 calibre bullets into it to see what happened. From this experiment the jury learned that the bullet which had killed Janet could not have struck the wall or it would have been flattened. The bullet had been found intact.

To get the lay of the land, the jury was driven out to the Osler Street home. As coroner Dr. Brydone-Jack led them downstairs, by coincidence Wong was ironing clothes in the laundry room just where Janet had fallen. The hapless houseboy was persuaded to lie down on the floor to show the position in which he'd found the body.

In the courtroom a gaggle of nervous, giggling nursemaids, friends of Janet, waited to testify. One fainted as her name was called. "Janet was definitely afraid of the Chinaman," testified Jean Brown Haddon, one of the nursemaids. "Once she told me the Chinaman squeezed her hand!" A gasp went through the predominately female audience. "He said her hand felt cold."

But Dr. Brydone-Jack produced two bank savings books in which Janet had kept her diary; they showed, he said, no evidence that her relations with Wong were anything but cordial. One entry read: "Poor Wong. He must be in love. He gave me a silk nightie and two camisoles." Another entry mentioned he'd helped her preserve strawberries.

Janet seemed to be much more interested in the constant round of young men she'd had passing acquaintance with, some of whom she'd met during her walks in Stanley Park. She was engaged to Arthur Dawson, a Roberts Creek lumber worker, but this didn't seem to have inhibited her flirtations.

Crowds came to hear the testimony of Wong who, in the atmosphere of hostility towards Orientals, was suspect No. 1. One member of the legislature, Mary Ellen Smith, with Wong's presumed guilt in mind, had even introduced a bill in the House to prevent white women working in homes where Chinese were employed.

After taking the "chicken oath," swearing on his ancestors to tell the truth, Wong gave a cool and consistent story of his actions. That fatal Saturday he had seen Janet three times; going upstairs, going out to hang up the baby clothes and going down to the basement with a basket of washing to iron. He had not seen her when he went downstairs for a smoke, he said, because his room was in another part of the basement away from the laundry room. After hearing the shot, he'd called her and then run downstairs. As he leaned over her inert body, her head moved a little and she seemed to be trying to say something, he said. He raised her head a little, then ran to phone Baker and to phone his uncle in Chinatown, presumably to ask his advice.

Yes, he admitted, the bottom of his apron had been covered with blood from bending over Janet, and he'd removed the stains by soaking it in cold water overnight.

"How did you know how to get the bloodstains out? asked Henderson.

"I learned that when I worked in Sun Mee Lung's laundry," he replied. At the conclusion of the week-long inquest, the jury decided that Janet had been murdered, "shot through the head by a revolver, by whom we have no evidence to show." But that settled nothing. In the legislature, Attorney-General Manson was under constant fire from the opposition for a supposed cover-up. In fact, he was bearing down on the police almost every day to take action, and opposition members, eventually learning the facts of the investigation, apologized.

Rumours swept the city that this or that public figure was involved. The name of Jack Nichol, the playboy son of the lieutenant-governor, was much bandied about, but he had been on a train to Calgary the day of the murder. For the most part, suspicion still centred on Wong Foon Sing.

Then on March 20, 1925, shortly after the Bakers had gone out to dinner for the evening, Wong, getting dressed in his street clothes in the basement, heard a dog barking. He looked out of the window but saw nothing, locked up his room and left the house. But as he looked back, he saw a light on in the basement. He returned, opened the door and called, "Who's there?" Suddenly hands reached out and grabbed him. Three men roughly handcuffed, blind-folded and gagged him, then carried him out to a car.

They drove, it seemed, for hours and Wong, cowering in the back, wondered if every minute would be his last. They crossed a long bridge and Wong, thinking he heard immi-gration officers' voices, assumed they were in the States; finally the car stopped and he was hustled into a house. When they took the blindfold off, Wong found himself sit-ting in a chair confronted by a circle of men. They were wearing the white sheets and hoods of the Ku Klux Klan.

"All right, you little bastard," came the muffled voice of their leader. "Now you're going to tell us how you mur-dered that girl." Lights flashed in the houseboy's head as he was knocked off the chair with a vicious blow.

"Tell us," a voice said, and a heavy boot smashed into his stomach.

The next day Baker reported to the police that Wong had disappeared. Ships leaving for China were searched, but no trace of him was found, and suspicion grew around the slim, young Oriental.

Meanwhile Wong was living a life of torment. During his forty-two-day imprisonment he was beaten regularly and threatened with death. At one point a noose was put around his neck and he was hoisted briefly off his feet. Another time a stranger who appeared to be a doctor felt his pulse. "He's dying," he said.

"Then we'll drop him in a hole and no one will be the wiser," said another voice. His captors were remarkably well informed, using a complete transcript of the inquest hearings to question him. But still Wong refused to confess.

The Chinese community, believing that dirty business was going on, offered a $500 reward for the discovery of Wong Foon Sing. At 3:00 A.M. on May 1, Wong was found by Sergeant Neil McPherson of the Point Grey police wandering on Marine Drive, his eyes still blindfolded after having been dumped off a few minutes before. If he thought his ordeal was over, he was wrong: the police immediately charged him with the murder of Janet Smith.

The plot began to thicken. Vancouver newspapers reported that Scotland Yard was working on a British angle; because of Baker's involvement in pharmaceutical drugs, there were rumours that drug smuggling was behind the murder. Then a Vancouver scandal sheet, the *Saturday Tribune,* published allegations by Barbara Orford, a local freelance writer, that a wild party had taken place in the Baker house the night before the murder. Baker, who had actually gone to bed exhausted at 9:30 that night after his tennis match, sued *Tribune* publisher J. Sedgwick Cowper. Eventually Miss Orford admitted that the scene had only taken place in one of her dreams.

The Chinese community increased a reward for the apprehension of Wong Foon Sing's abductors to $3,000. Finally a break came. One of the men in on the scheme, appropriately named Verity Norton, squealed. Headlines screamed, and one newspaper had a special edition on the streets within an hour of the arrest by provincial police of O.B.V. Robinson, the owner of the Canadian Detective Agency. The next day, his seventeen-year-old son William was also arrested. Robinson had worked on the case earlier for the attorney-general and had been working for the municipality of Point Grey while he masterminded the kidnapping. But that was only the beginning. Point Grey's police chief, John Murdoch, a sergeant, Percy Kirkham, two police commissioners and two officials of the Scottish Societies were also charged with abduction. *Tribune* publisher Cowper, also charged, turned out to be the man who had taken Wong's pulse, pretending to be a doctor.

In court Norton related all the details of the kidnapping plan, including a notion that the abductors would hypnotize Wong. The houseboy, taken to a home about a kilometre away from Osler Street on West 25th Avenue, was able to identify the room where he had been chained. And a local grocer identified Robinson, the private detective, as the man who'd come into his store throughout the kidnap period to buy canned goods, "never any vegetables."

In the flurry of charges and countercharges that followed, Robinson was sentenced to a year in jail, Norton got nine months and the rest went free. Cowper finally had to pay the Bakers $2,000 for libel. At the fall assizes the grand jury brought in "no bill" against Wong, who had suffered permanent damage to one ear drum from the beatings. That meant there was not enough evidence to go ahead with a trial, and that was the end of it.

No one to this day knows who killed Janet Smith. "I think it was a Society cover-up all the way," Jack Nilan, a veteran reporter who covered some of the hearings, told me. But Cecil Clark, retired deputy commissioner of the provincial police, was familiar with the investigation and the officers involved at the time, and tells me it was what it appears to be: a complete mystery.

The facts point to two possible conclusions: the murderer was either Wong Foon Sing or someone very familiar with the Baker home; for how would an outsider have known of the existence of the gun? An argument or a spiteful remark by Janet might have sparked the houseboy's anger, but his long and faultless service to the family and his persistence in maintaining his innocence in the face of torture and beatings suggest otherwise.

If someone else killed Janet, how did he get down to the

basement, and where was he when Wong heard the shot and ran downstairs? Some have suggested Janet's body was moved to the basement after she was killed, accounting for the peculiar position in which the body was found, with the head under the tub, but that would have exposed the killer to the risk of being seen by Wong.

As to a motive, it could have been the jealousy of one of her boyfriends, or perhaps the jealousy of Wong. Or had she become pregnant by someone whose prominent position made it imperative that this fact be concealed? If so, the hurried embalming of the body is significant; afterwards the pathologist was unable to determine whether or not she was pregnant.

The alibis of everyone in the case except Wong are almost suspiciously cast-iron, leaving one to wonder whether, as in the Christine Demeter murder in Toronto in 1973, a killer had been hired to do away with Janet.

We shall never know: the cedar-shingled house still stands on Osler Street keeping its secret.

It was just getting dark on a February afternoon when I found Janet Smith's grave in Mountain View Cemetery, and I had to get down on my knees to make out the inscription on the granite cairn erected by the Scottish Societies of British Columbia:

> In loving memory of Janet K. Smith who met her death while in the bloom of youth at Shaughnessy Heights on July 26th, 1924, aged 22 years, one month and one day.
>
> On earth one gentle soul the less,
> In Heaven one angel more.

On March 6, 1926, Wong Foon Sing climbed the gang-plank of the *Empress of Russia,* bound for China. As the ship sailed from Vancouver's spectacular harbour at midnight, Wong leaned over the rail looking back at the city's disappearing lights. And if he felt a wave of relief at leaving Canadian soil, who can blame him?

The Nightmare
of Paul Stromkins

He had but to close his eyes and the unspeakable thing rose before him again—that fellow Baker with his scrawny neck and that clean-cut young kid who could have been his own son. He saw the two boats pitching in the Georgia Strait, Baker and young Sowash leaning over the bodies lying on the deck, leaning over with the knife and—

"Dad, Dad, wake up! What's the matter with you?" his wife cried. "You shouted in your sleep again."

"Oh, Mother, I can't tell you," he said, turning to the wall. And as he thought of the proud day long ago in Manitoba when they'd made him a justice of the peace, a sob rose in his throat. "That I should come to this. That I should have blood on my hands," he thought to himself.

When Paul Stromkins had left the harsh Manitoba winters behind for the soft green climate of Vancouver Island, it had seemed as though six months of life had been added to every year. He'd bought a fishing boat, learned the ways of the sea, and everything had been going well—at least until that day when the two strangers, the fellow with the Adam's apple bobbing in his skinny neck and the kid who might have been a football player, perched on the dock and asked him casually if he'd care to charter his boat.

"Well, that would depend. . . ." he'd said.

All night the memory churned through his mind. If only . . . The next morning, a Sunday, he couldn't sit still. He tried to busy himself with jobs in the yard of their neat little house just up from the water, but his wife could see his mind was elsewhere. And when the knock came at the door just after lunch, he was jumpier than ever. "Mr. Stromkins?" said the policeman—he knew it was going to be a policeman—"We'd like you to come down to the head-quarters to answer a few questions." Stromkins's hands shook as he tried to tie his shoelaces.

In the business of apprehending murderers, remorse is often the policeman's best friend. Where microscopes, fingerprint experts and the skill of the best detectives all fail, a troubled conscience will often crack the toughest murder case wide open. That's the way it was with Stromkins, whose involvement in a brutal double murder at sea off Vancouver Island would haunt him until the day he died.

Vancouver Island, pointing like a finger into United States territory, and blessed with thousands of secret coves and picturesque little offshore islands, has for generations tempted smugglers wanting to spirit illicit goods into the States. In the last century, Victoria was the biggest opium distribution centre on the Pacific coast, with half a dozen opium factories operating openly with government licences to supply the Chinese market in California. In the last couple of decades, this rugged coastline has attracted drug smugglers bringing in marijuana and hard drugs on small boats from Mexico. But in the 1920s, smuggling booze into prohibition-era America was a major industry in these parts.

Rusty old freighters bearing libations from the distilleries of Scotland would lumber to the edge of Canadian waters where small Canadian vessels, quite legally, would shuttle the goods to caches on shore or transfer them to high-speed launches operated with relative impunity by American smugglers. These remarkable vessels, called "fast freighters," consisted of long, hollow hulls powered by two V-8 aircraft engines that would skim across the waves, landing the stuff on American soil almost before United States customs officials could turn their slower vessels around to give chase.

This profitable business attracted not only unscrupulous men ready to break American laws, but also rash desperados daring enough to try to steal from the rum runners. Men like Owen B. Baker, a gangling, uncoordinated sort of fellow whose hayseed image lasted only until you noticed the hard, shrewd eyes. Baker ambled into a Seattle firm of haberdashers in August 1924 and picked out a yachtsman's cap and eight brass buttons.

"Any particular insignia?" asked the clerk, Harold Kerrigan, thinking he was a ship's officer. "What line?"

"Line, hell!" laughed Baker. "I'm running booze out of Canada. I want this cap to look like a revenue officer's." Baker, who left the store with the cap weighted down with an admiral's quota of gold trim, hadn't told the clerk the whole story.

His game, which worked successfully several times, was to arrive with his official cap and blazer, a flashlight, revolvers and phony police badge just as rum runners were unloading their illegal cargo on the beaches of Puget Sound. "United States Customs," he'd shout. "Stay where you are!" And with any luck the rum runners would take off, leaving Baker with their cargo.

One time Baker pulled the same trick on a man who had stopped at a traffic light in Tacoma, Washington, with four cases of booze in the back of his car. Baker drove up, flashed his badge, handcuffed the unfortunate man to his own steering wheel, and took off with the liquor. Then, walking along a Seattle street, Baker had the misfortune to run right into three powerful men to whom he had sold ten cases of gin that had turned out to be water. Baker looked aghast when they told him of the mistake. "You don't say!" he said. "Well it just happens the guy who sold me that gin is around the corner. I'll get him."

And Baker took off at a brisk trot for the Commodore Hotel where, oddly enough, the three strong men found him shortly afterwards looking for his old pal in a pile of sawdust in which he had unaccountably buried himself. The three invited him upstairs to a fourth-floor room where, jokers all, they suspended Baker out of the window by his heels until he gave them back their money.

After that Baker decided a bit of sea air might do him good and invited an old friend, Harry Sowash, along. "Si" Sowash, aged twenty-three, with crew cut and husky build, could have been taken for a college boy, and he had a delightful sense of humour. But his career to that point had hardly been distinguished: in Honolulu, while in the United States army, he had struck a sergeant with a shovel and had later been caught selling aircraft parts. Baker and Sowash's mutual alma mater was the McNeill Island Penitentiary where Baker, aged thirty-nine, had been serving a term for white slaving.

It was this pair, along with a buddy, Charlie Morris, who engaged Paul Stromkins's boat, the *Denman II,* for some highly specialized fishing—seeking out hidden caches of liquor along the coast which they could steal. For a week Stromkins cruised the south coast of Vancouver Island with his three customers staying mostly below in the cabin, but they found nothing. Then one hazy afternoon they passed a cannery boat chugging along off Sooke Harbour.

"What's that boat?" Baker shouted up from the cabin.

"She's the *Beryl G,*" said Stromkins at the wheel. "She's shuttling liquor from a freighter out in international waters. Likely she's unloading her stuff into one of Pete Marinoff's fast freighters." Marinoff's "fast freighters" were famous in these waters. Originally an Austrian immigrant, he owned eleven of the specially designed launches that could streak across the water at seventy-five kilometres per hour or more.

"Oh you Daddy! I'd like to get some of that liquor," Stromkins heard Baker say with a chuckle to the other two.

The *Beryl G,* the object of Baker's avarice, was operated by Bill Gillis and his seventeen-year-old son, Bill, Jr., and it was named after his daughter, Beryl. Lugging cases of liquor at $6 a case to a quiet spot where Marinoff's boats could pick them up seemed an easy way of making a living, but Bill Gillis, a big, jovial man with friends all up and down the coast, was under no illusions—sharks of the human sort lurked in these waters.

The *Beryl G* was moored off Sidney Island the night of September 15, and the father and son had not long finished their supper when young Bill shouted down, "Dad, there's a dinghy coming our way." Taking no chances, Gillis reached for his .303 rifle and climbed the companionway. A man was coming over the side wearing a uniform, cap and blue blazer. "Customs! Stay where you are," he cried.

"Customs, hell," said big Bill Gillis.

* * *

Two days later Chris Waters, a lighthouse keeper at Turn Point on the American side of Haro Strait, spotted a boat that seemed to be drifting with the tide. With another man he set off in his boat, and as they came closer they made out the name on the bow: *Beryl G.* No one seemed to be aboard, so they took her in tow, brought her into harbour and then went on board. This was no sea-caused disaster: everywhere they looked there was blood. It splattered the decks, led down the companionway. When they clambered down into the cabin they found everything scattered and broken as though there'd been a violent struggle. On top of an open magazine lay an engineer's hat soaked in blood. Of the father and son there was no sign.

The British Columbia Provincial Police went over the *Beryl G* with a fine-tooth comb. Among their finds were a number of .303 cartridges, a yachtman's hat and a camera. When the film in the camera was developed, it showed the *Beryl G* and one of Marinoff's fast launches: young Gillis, apparently, had been taking photographs of their rum-running operation for a souvenir. Marinoff, who had cordial enough relations with British Columbia authorities, confirmed that the *Beryl G* had been delivering goods to his boys. In fact, he was able to pinpoint the time of the *Beryl G*'s disappearance because she had failed to turn up for a rendezvous off Sidney Island.

Weeks of checking on both sides of the border produced this information: two characters named Sowash and Baker had recently hired a Seattle vessel to pick up liquor they had cached on Canadian islands and which they had sold in Seattle. The liquor brands coincided with those the *Beryl G* was carrying. Sowash and Baker had long since disappeared, but the police got a hint that Paul Stromkins had been involved. "No way," Stromkins protested when he was questioned the first time. "I was working at home that day." But the police suspected that sooner or later Stromkins would yield to questioning.

Cecil "Nobby" Clark, the former deputy commissioner of the provincial police who has recorded his memories of those stirring days in his book, *Tales of the British Columbia Police*, recalled for me the moment when Stromkins broke. "It was a Sunday afternoon and everything was quiet and still in the building where we had the police headquarters," said Clark, who today lives just up the road from where Stromkins used to moore the *Denman II* at the Royal Victoria Yacht Club. Assistant Commissioner Walter Owen told a constable to bring Stromkins in for questioning, and soon afterwards the nervous-looking fisherman was ushered into the room.

"I was just a young policeman taking everything down," said Clark, "and I have never heard a more masterful interrogation. The voices were so quiet you could hardly hear them."

"Do you remember what you were doing on September 15?" asked Owens. "Now turn your mind back and see if you can remember."

"Oh yes," said Stromkins, "I was home all day."

"What were you doing?"

"Well, I was working about the place."

"Did you need any nails?" The voice was dangerously quiet.

"Yeh, I think I did. I got them in Victoria."

"What street?"

"I don't remember."

"Did you go in on the streetcar?"

"Yeh, that's it."

"Was it the Island hardware store?"

"Yeh, that's right."

"Constable," said Owens, "go and check with that store if Mr. Stromkins bought nails that day."

"We knew, you see," said Clark, "that Stromkins had made a long distance phone call to his home from Sidney Island that day."

"Now," said Owens, "I want you to study this calendar and make sure of the dates." Stromkins's growing agitation was visible. "Now," said Owens, reaching into his desk drawer. "I want you to take a look at these pictures. Do you know these men?" he asked, sliding photographs of Sowash and Baker across the desk.

Stromkins gave them only a glance. Then, said Clark, "he covered his face with his hands and the tears were running out between his fingers." He let out a wail. "Oh my God! To think," he said, "that only yesterday my little baby won a prize in the baby show." And after that, said Clark, they couldn't stop him talking.

The evening of the murders, Baker, Sowash and Morris had come aboard the *Denman II*. Baker, carrying a black zippered bag, had told Stromkins they were going out to Sidney Island after the *Beryl G*. They arrived there late in the evening and Baker opened the bag, pulled out his fancy hat, some handcuffs and several revolvers.

"You don't need those. They will only lead to trouble," said the frightened Stromkins.

"Aw, shut up!" snapped Baker. "Those guys will cave in right away. There won't be no shooting."

While Stromkins stayed behind, the three men rowed over to the *Beryl G* in Stromkins's small rowboat. But almost the second Baker went over the side, Stromkins saw his gun blaze in the darkness, and a few minutes later Baker rowed back furiously to the *Denman II*. "Come up alongside and lash your boat to the *Beryl G*," he ordered.

Without further explanation, they began transferring the *Beryl G*'s cargo to the *Denman II*. "We had to shoot the old man," Morris told Stromkins out of the corner of his mouth as they transferred the load. "We shot him a little in the arm."

It was light as the two boats, still lashed together, headed for Bear Island to stash the liquor. Stromkins saw young Bill Gillis emerge dazed onto the deck of the *Beryl G*. "He got one step outside when Sowash hit him on the head and he fell," Stromkins was to testify. Then, as Baker and Sowash went below to drag Captain Gillis onto the deck, Stromkins saw young Bill Gillis move. At Baker and Sowash's trial months later, Stromkins collapsed in the stand when he got to that part of the story. Baker, he said between sobs, had handcuffed the father and son together. Then he had taken out a knife and ripped them open so that the bodies would sink.

A lawyer moved in to ask a question about that awful moment. "Oh my God—don't talk about it," he moaned, sinking forward in the witness box and weeping. "Get away from me. You are worse than Baker, asking all those questions." In the prisoners' dock, Baker smiled broadly.

Then Stromkins proceeded to tell the crowded courtroom how Baker and Sowash, after pitching the two bodies overboard attached to an anchor, stood on the blood-soaked deck of the *Beryl G* and shook hands in triumph.

"The cold-blooded murderers!" Morris had hissed as he and Stromkins watched from the *Denman II*. Later, as Stromkins was about to drop the three men off at Anacortes on the American side, Baker told him: "If you say anything, we'll all hang together."

It took a continentwide manhunt to apprehend Sowash

and Baker. Sowash was picked up in a sweep of the New Orleans waterfront by local police, and Baker was arrested working on a dredge in New York harbour. On the way back to Victoria, Sowash obligingly wrote a confession—putting nearly all the blame on his old buddy Baker. "Here," he said, handing the confession to a police inspector. "A good caption for that might be, 'The Toilers of the Sea.' "

At Okalla prison, Sowash was caught trying to swing a copy of the confession across to Baker's cell on a thread. He had carefully marked in the margins what Baker should say so that their statements would coincide. But when the two men got in court, each tried to accuse the other. "It was as if they were each trying to push the other into the abyss," said Clark. Not even the tearful testimony of Baker's eighty-year-old mother, his wife and his little boy, that he had been nowhere near Vancouver Island the day of the murder, was enough to save the scoundrel, and both he and Sowash were sentenced to death, with Morris eventually getting a life sentence.

Baker passed his last days writing to relations and friends, pleading for money and legal help to launch a last-minute appeal. The laconic Sowash wrote only one letter. It was to the manufacturer of a shaving cream who had just then come up with a new sales gimmick—a little chain to prevent the container cap from falling off. Tongue in cheek, Sowash wrote that for years he had been troubled by the cap falling down the sink when he shaved, and he had nothing but praise for this bold new innovation. He made no mention of the fact that he didn't expect to be shaving for much longer.

Baker and Sowash were hanged on November 4, 1925, and author and journalist Bruce Hutchinson, who covered the trial, recalled that Baker, a little presumptuously, declared on the scaffold, "Jesus died for others, and so do I."

But murders are never finished. It doesn't quite end when the police go away, when the judge (in days gone by) puts on the black hat or when the prison gates close behind the convicted killer. So deeply affecting are murders to those having even a remote connection with them that the aftereffects reverberate for years to come.

And Paul Stromkins was no exception. His wife, a hale ninety-one when I spoke to her in Victoria, recalled that even as he lay dying in 1975, her husband would start up in his sleep and cry, "The trial! The trial! Oh, goodness, it's going to be soon."

"No, no, Dad, she would comfort him. Hush now, it's not going to come."